MznLnx

Missing Links Exam Preps

Exam Prep for

Marketing Research

Hair et al..., 3rd Edition

The MznLnx Exam Prep is your link from the texbook and lecture to your exams.
The MznLnx Exam Preps are unauthorized and comprehensive reviews of your textbooks.

All material provided by MznLnx and Rico Publications (c) 2010
Textbook publishers and textbook authors do not particpate in or contribute to these reviews.

MznLnx

Rico Publications

Exam Prep for Marketing Research
3rd Edition
Hair et al...

Publisher: Raymond Houge
Assistant Editor: Michael Rouger
Text and Cover Designer: Lisa Buckner
Marketing Manager: Sara Swagger
Project Manager, Editorial Production: Jerry Emerson
Art Director: Vernon Lowerui

Product Manager: Dave Mason
Editorial Assitant: Rachel Guzmanji
Pedagogy: Debra Long
Cover Image: Jim Reed/Getty Images
Text and Cover Printer: City Printing, Inc.
Compositor: Media Mix, Inc.

(c) 2010 Rico Publications
ALL RIGHTS RESERVED. No part of this work covered by the copyright may be reproduced or used in any form or by an means--graphic, electronic, or mechanical, including photocopying, recording, taping, Web distribution, information storage, and retrieval systems, or in any other manner--without the written permission of the publisher.

Printed in the United States
ISBN:

For more information about our products, contact us at:
Dave.Mason@RicoPublications.com

For permission to use material from this text or product, submit a request online to:
Dave.Mason@RicoPublications.com

Contents

CHAPTER 1
Marketing Research for Managerial Decision Making — 1

CHAPTER 2
The Marketing Research Process — 20

CHAPTER 3
Information Management for Marketing Decisions: Secondary Data Sources — 30

CHAPTER 4
Customer Relationship Management and the Marketing Research Process — 42

CHAPTER 5
Marketing Decision Support Systems — 52

CHAPTER 6
Exploratory Designs: In-Depth Interviews and Focus Groups — 62

CHAPTER 7
Descriptive Research Designs: Survey Methods and Errors — 72

CHAPTER 8
Observation Techniques, Experiments, and Test Markets — 83

CHAPTER 9
Sampling: Theory and Design — 94

CHAPTER 10
Sampling: Methods and Planning — 102

CHAPTER 11
Overview of Measurement: Construct Development and Scale Measurement — 110

CHAPTER 12
Attitude Scale Measurements Used in Marketing Research — 118

CHAPTER 13
Questionnaire Design and Issues — 126

CHAPTER 14
Coding, Editing, and Preparing Data for Analysis — 133

CHAPTER 15
Data Analysis: Testing for Significant Differences — 138

CHAPTER 16
Data Analysis: Testing for Association — 148

CHAPTER 17
Data Analysis: Multivariate Techniques for the Research Process — 154

CHAPTER 18
Preparing the Marketing Research Report and Presentation — 163

ANSWER KEY — 167

TO THE STUDENT

COMPREHENSIVE

The *MznLnx* Exam Prep series is designed to help you pass your exams. Editors at MznLnx review your textbooks and then prepare these practice exams to help you master the textbook material. Unlike study guides, workbooks, and practice tests provided by the texbook publisher and textbook authors, *MznLnx* gives you **all** of the material in each chapter in exam form, not just samples, so you can be sure to nail your exam.

MECHANICAL

The MznLnx Exam Prep series creates exams that will help you learn the subject matter as well as test you on your understanding. Each question is designed to help you master the concept. Just working through the exams, you gain an understanding of the subject--its a simple mechanical process that produces success.

INTEGRATED STUDY GUIDE AND REVIEW

MznLnx is not just a set of exams designed to test you, its also a comprehensive review of the subject content. Each exam question is also a review of the concept, making sure that you will get the answer correct without having to go to other sources of material. You learn as you go! Its the easiest way to pass an exam.

HUMOR

Studying can be tedious and dry. MznLnx's instructional design includes moderate humor within the exam questions on occassion, to break the tedium and revitalize the brain

Chapter 1. Marketing Research for Managerial Decision Making

1. The _____ is a professional association for marketers. As of 2008 it had approximately 40,000 members. There are collegiate chapters on 250 campuses.
   - a. ACNielsen
   - b. ADTECH
   - c. AMAX
   - d. American Marketing Association

2. _____ is a branch of philosophy which seeks to address questions about morality, such as how a moral outcome can be achieved in a specific situation (applied _____), how moral values should be determined (normative _____), what moral values people actually abide by (descriptive _____), what the fundamental semantic, ontological, and epistemic nature of _____ or morality is (meta-_____), and how moral capacity or moral agency develops and what its nature is (moral psychology.)

   Socrates was one of the first Greek philosophers to encourage both scholars and the common citizen to turn their attention from the outside world to the condition of man. In this view, Knowledge having a bearing on human life was placed highest, all other knowledge being secondary.

   - a. ACNielsen
   - b. ADTECH
   - c. AMAX
   - d. Ethics

3. _____ is defined by the American _____ Association as the activity, set of institutions, and processes for creating, communicating, delivering, and exchanging offerings that have value for customers, clients, partners, and society at large. The term developed from the original meaning which referred literally to going to market, as in shopping, or going to a market to sell goods or services.

   _____ practice tends to be seen as a creative industry, which includes advertising, distribution and selling.

   - a. Marketing myopia
   - b. Marketing
   - c. Customer acquisition management
   - d. Product naming

4. Consumer market research is a form of applied sociology that concentrates on understanding the behaviours, whims and preferences, of consumers in a market-based economy, and aims to understand the effects and comparative success of marketing campaigns. The field of consumer _____ as a statistical science was pioneered by Arthur Nielsen with the founding of the ACNielsen Company in 1923.

   Thus _____ is the systematic and objective identification, collection, analysis, and dissemination of information for the purpose of assisting management in decision making related to the identification and solution of problems and opportunities in marketing.

   - a. Marketing research process
   - b. Marketing research
   - c. Focus group
   - d. Logit analysis

5. _____ is the ability of an individual or group to seclude themselves or information about themselves and thereby reveal themselves selectively. The boundaries and content of what is considered private differ among cultures and individuals, but share basic common themes. _____ is sometimes related to anonymity, the wish to remain unnoticed or unidentified in the public realm.
   - a. Power III
   - b. 180SearchAssistant
   - c. Privacy
   - d. 6-3-5 Brainwriting

6. _____ consists of the processes a company uses to track and organize its contacts with its current and prospective customers. _____ software is used to support these processes; information about customers and customer interactions can be entered, stored and accessed by employees in different company departments. Typical _____ goals are to improve services provided to customers, and to use customer contact information for targeted marketing.
   a. Demand generation
   b. Product bundling
   c. Customer relationship management
   d. Commercialization

7. A _____ is a retail establishment which specializes in selling a wide range of products without a single predominant merchandise line. _____s usually sell products including apparel, furniture, appliances, electronics, and additionally select other lines of products such as paint, hardware, toiletries, cosmetics, photographic equipment, jewelery, toys, and sporting goods. Certain _____s are further classified as discount _____s.
   a. 6-3-5 Brainwriting
   b. 180SearchAssistant
   c. Power III
   d. Department Store

8. _____ is a form of marketing developed from direct response marketing campaigns conducted in the 1970's and 1980's which emphasizes customer retention and satisfaction, rather than a dominant focus on 'point of sale' transactions.

_____ differs from other forms of marketing in that it recognizes the long term value to the firm of keeping customers, as opposed to direct or 'Intrusion' marketing, which focuses upon acquisition of new clients by targeting majority demographics based upon prospective client lists.

_____ refers to long-term and mutually beneficial arrangement wherein both buyer and seller focus on value enhancement through the certain of more satisfying exchange. This approach attempts to transcend the simple purchase exchange process with customer to make more meaningful and richer contact by providing a more holistic, personalized purchase, and use orn consumption experience to create stronger ties.

   a. Guerrilla Marketing
   b. Global marketing
   c. Relationship marketing
   d. Diversity marketing

9. Customer _____ consists of the processes a company uses to track and organize its contacts with its current and prospective customers. CRelationship management software is used to support these processes; information about customers and customer interactions can be entered, stored and accessed by employees in different company departments. Typical CRelationship management goals are to improve services provided to customers, and to use customer contact information for targeted marketing.
   a. Green marketing
   b. Product bundling
   c. Marketing
   d. Relationship management

10. In statistics, _____ is a simple measure of the variability or dispersion of a data set. A low _____ indicates that the data points tend to be very close to the same value (the mean), while high _____ indicates that the data are 'spread out' over a large range of values.

For example, the average height for adult men in the United States is about 70 inches, with a _____ of around 3 inches.

Chapter 1. Marketing Research for Managerial Decision Making

a. Pearson product-moment correlation coefficient
c. Z-test
b. Standard deviation
d. Statistically significant

11. In mathematics, an _____, or central tendency of a data set refers to a measure of the 'middle' or 'expected' value of the data set. There are many different descriptive statistics that can be chosen as a measurement of the central tendency of the data items.

An _____ is a single value that is meant to typify a list of values.

a. ACNielsen
c. ADTECH
b. AMAX
d. Average

12. _____ is a set of six steps which defines the tasks to be accomplished in conducting a marketing research study. These include problem definition, developing an approach to problem, research design formulation, field work, data preparation and analysis, and report generation and presentation.
a. Market analysis
c. Marketing research process
b. Preference-rank translation
d. Simple random sampling

13. _____ refer to a collection of facts usually collected as the result of experience, observation or experiment or a set of premises. This may consist of numbers, words particularly as measurements or observations of a set of variables. _____ are often viewed as a lowest level of abstraction from which information and knowledge are derived.
a. Data
c. Pearson product-moment correlation coefficient
b. Sample size
d. Mean

14. _____ is a term used to describe a process of preparing and collecting data - for example as part of a process improvement or similar project.

_____ usually takes place early on in an improvement project, and is often formalised through a _____ Plan which often contains the following activity.

1. Pre collection activity - Agree goals, target data, definitions, methods
2. Collection - _____
3. Present Findings - usually involves some form of sorting analysis and/or presentation.

A formal _____ process is necessary as it ensures that data gathered is both defined and accurate and that subsequent decisions based on arguments embodied in the findings are valid. The process provides both a baseline from which to measure from and in certain cases a target on what to improve. Types of _____ 1-By mail questionnaires 2-By personal interview

- Six sigma
- Sampling (statistics)

a. 6-3-5 Brainwriting
b. Data collection
c. 180SearchAssistant
d. Power III

15. _____ is the process of extracting hidden patterns from data. As more data is gathered, with the amount of data doubling every three years, _____ is becoming an increasingly important tool to transform this data into information. It is commonly used in a wide range of profiling practices, such as marketing, surveillance, fraud detection and scientific discovery.
   a. Data mining
   b. 180SearchAssistant
   c. Structure mining
   d. Power III

16. A _____ is a structured collection of records or data that is stored in a computer system. The structure is achieved by organizing the data according to a _____ model. The model in most common use today is the relational model.
   a. 6-3-5 Brainwriting
   b. 180SearchAssistant
   c. Power III
   d. Database

17. A _____ is a research instrument consisting of a series of questions and other prompts for the purpose of gathering information from respondents. Although they are often designed for statistical analysis of the responses, this is not always the case. The _____ was invented by Sir Francis Galton.
   a. Market research
   b. Mystery shoppers
   c. Mystery shopping
   d. Questionnaire

18. _____ is that part of statistical practice concerned with the selection of individual observations intended to yield some knowledge about a population of concern, especially for the purposes of statistical inference. Each observation measures one or more properties (weight, location, etc.) of an observable entity enumerated to distinguish objects or individuals.
   a. Sampling
   b. Richard Buckminster 'Bucky' Fuller
   c. AStore
   d. Sports Marketing Group

19. Combining Existing _____ Sources with New Primary Data Sources

Imagine that we could get hold of a good collection of surveys taken in earlier years, such as detailed studies about changes going on in this phase and hopefully additional studies in the years to come. Analyzing this data base over time could give us a good picture of what changes actually have taken place in the orientation of the population and of the extent to which new technical concepts did have an impact on subgroups of the population. Furthermore, data archives can help to prepare studies on change over time by monitoring what questions have been asked in earlier years and alerting principal investigators to important questions which should be repeated in planned research projects.

   a. Power III
   b. 180SearchAssistant
   c. 6-3-5 Brainwriting
   d. Secondary data

Chapter 1. Marketing Research for Managerial Decision Making   5

20. _____ is a marketing term, and involves evaluating the situation and trends in a particular company's market. _____ is often called the 'three c's', which refers to the three major elements that must be studied:

- Customers
- Costs
- Competition

The number of 'c's' is sometimes extended to four, five, or even six, with 'Collaboration', 'Company', and 'Competitive advantage'.

- Marketing mix
- SWOT analysis

   a. 180SearchAssistant   b. 6-3-5 Brainwriting
   c. Situation analysis   d. Power III

21. _____ a research method involving the use of questionnaires and/or statistical surveys to gather data about people and their thoughts and behaviours.
   a. T-test   b. Survey research
   c. Z-test   d. Control chart

22. In marketing, customer _____, lifetime customer value (LCV), or _____ (LTV) and a new concept of 'customer life cycle management' is the present value of the future cash flows attributed to the customer relationship. Use of customer _____ as a marketing metric tends to place greater emphasis on customer service and long-term customer satisfaction, rather than on maximizing short-term sales.

Customer _____ has intuitive appeal as a marketing concept, because in theory it represents exactly how much each customer is worth in monetary terms, and therefore exactly how much a marketing department should be willing to spend to acquire each customer.

   a. Value chain   b. Brand infiltration
   c. Sweepstakes   d. Lifetime value

23. _____ in organizations and public policy is both the organizational process of creating and maintaining a plan; and the psychological process of thinking about the activities required to create a desired goal on some scale. As such, it is a fundamental property of intelligent behavior. This thought process is essential to the creation and refinement of a plan, or integration of it with other plans, that is, it combines forecasting of developments with the preparation of scenarios of how to react to them.
   a. 6-3-5 Brainwriting   b. Planning
   c. Power III   d. 180SearchAssistant

24. A personal and cultural _____ is a relative ethic _____, an assumption upon which implementation can be extrapolated. A _____ system is a set of consistent _____s and measures that is soo not true. A principle _____ is a foundation upon which other _____s and measures of integrity are based.

a. Perceptual maps
c. Package-on-Package
b. Supreme Court of the United States
d. Value

25. _____ is a rivalry between individuals, groups, nations for territory, a niche, or allocation of resources. It arises whenever two or more parties strive for a goal which cannot be shared. _____ occurs naturally between living organisms which co-exist in the same environment.

a. Price fixing
c. Price competition
b. Competition
d. Non-price competition

26. A _____ is a subgroup of people or organizations sharing one or more characteristics that cause them to have similar product and/or service needs. A true _____ meets all of the following criteria: it is distinct from other segments (different segments have different needs), it is homogeneous within the segment (exhibits common needs); it responds similarly to a market stimulus, and it can be reached by a market intervention. The term is also used when consumers with identical product and/or service needs are divided up into groups so they can be charged different amounts.

a. Commercial planning
c. Production orientation
b. Customer insight
d. Market segment

27. Competitiveness is a comparative concept of the ability and performance of a firm, sub-sector or country to sell and supply goods and/or services in a given market. Although widely used in economics and business management, the usefulness of the concept, particularly in the context of national competitiveness, is vigorously disputed by economists, such as Paul Krugman .

The term may also be applied to markets, where it is used to refer to the extent to which the market structure may be regarded as perfectly _____.

a. Geographical pricing
c. Customs union
b. Free trade zone
d. Competitive

28. _____ was originally coined by Austrian psychologist Alfred Adler in 1929. The current broader sense of the word dates from 1961.

In sociology, a _____ is the way a person lives.

a. 180SearchAssistant
c. Power III
b. 6-3-5 Brainwriting
d. Lifestyle

29. A _____ is a documented investigation of a Market that is used to inform a firm's planning activities particularly around decision of: inventory, purchase, work force expansion/contraction, facility expansion, purchases of capital equipment, promotional activities, and many other aspects of a company.

Not all managers are asked to conduct a _____, but all managers must make decisions using _____ data and understand how the data was derived. So all managers need a reasonable understanding of the tools most used for making sales forecasts and analyzing markets.

a. Preference regression
c. Simple random sampling
b. Market analysis
d. Cross tabulation

30. _____ is a methodology in the social sciences for studying the content of communication. Earl Babbie defines it as 'the study of recorded human communications, such as books, websites, paintings and laws.' It is most commonly used by researchers in the social sciences to analyze recorded transcripts of interviews with participants.

_____ is also considered a scholarly methodology in the humanities by which texts are studied as to authorship, authenticity, of meaning.

a. 6-3-5 Brainwriting
c. Power III
b. 180SearchAssistant
d. Content analysis

31. In marketing, _____ has come to mean the process by which marketers try to create an image or identity in the minds of their target market for its product, brand, or organization. It is the 'relative competitive comparison' their product occupies in a given market as perceived by the target market.

Re-_____ involves changing the identity of a product, relative to the identity of competing products, in the collective minds of the target market.

a. Containerization
c. GE matrix
b. Moratorium
d. Positioning

32. A _____ applies the scientific method to experimentally examine an intervention in the real world (or as many experimental economists like to say, naturally-occurring environments) rather than in the laboratory. _____s, like lab experiments, generally randomize subjects (or other sampling units) into treatment and control groups and compare outcomes between these groups. Clinical trials of pharmaceuticals are one example of _____s.

a. Response variable
c. Power III
b. 180SearchAssistant
d. Field experiment

33. The _____ is generally accepted as the use and specification of the four p's describing the strategic position of a product in the marketplace. One version of the origins of the _____ starts in 1948 when James Culliton said that a marketing decision should be a result of something similar to a recipe. This version continued in 1953 when Neil Borden, in his American Marketing Association presidential address, took the recipe idea one step further and coined the term 'Marketing-Mix'.

a. 6-3-5 Brainwriting
c. Power III
b. 180SearchAssistant
d. Marketing mix

34. _____ is a graphics technique used by asset marketers that attempts to visually display the perceptions of customers or potential customers. Typically the position of a product, product line, brand, or company is displayed relative to their competition.

Perceptual maps can have any number of dimensions but the most common is two dimensions.

a. Perceptual mapping
c. Market environment
b. Kano model
d. Customer franchise

35. A number of different _____s are indicated below.

- Randomized controlled trial
    - Double-blind randomized trial
    - Single-blind randomized trial
    - Non-blind trial
- Nonrandomized trial (quasi-experiment)
    - Interrupted time series design (measures on a sample or a series of samples from the same population are obtained several times before and after a manipulated event or a naturally occurring event) - considered a type of quasi-experiment

- Cohort study
    - Prospective cohort
    - Retrospective cohort
    - Time series study
- Case-control study
    - Nested case-control study
- Cross-sectional study
    - Community survey (a type of cross-sectional study)

When choosing a _____, many factors must be taken into account. Different types of studies are subject to different types of bias. For example, recall bias is likely to occur in cross-sectional or case-control studies where subjects are asked to recall exposure to risk factors.

a. Power III
c. Longitudinal studies
b. 180SearchAssistant
d. Study design

36. _____ is an organization's process of defining its strategy and making decisions on allocating its resources to pursue this strategy, including its capital and people. Various business analysis techniques can be used in _____, including SWOT analysis (Strengths, Weaknesses, Opportunities, and Threats) and PEST analysis (Political, Economic, Social, and Technological analysis) or STEER analysis involving Socio-cultural, Technological, Economic, Ecological, and Regulatory factors and EPISTEL (Environment, Political, Informatic, Social, Technological, Economic and Legal)

_____ is the formal consideration of an organization's future course. All _____ deals with at least one of three key questions:

1. 'What do we do?'
2. 'For whom do we do it?'
3. 'How do we excel?'

In business _____, the third question is better phrased 'How can we beat or avoid competition?'. (Bradford and Duncan, page 1.)

a. 180SearchAssistant
b. Power III
c. 6-3-5 Brainwriting
d. Strategic planning

37. _____, a business term, is a measure of how products and services supplied by a company meet or surpass customer expectation. It is seen as a key performance indicator within business and is part of the four perspectives of a Balanced Scorecard.

In a competitive marketplace where businesses compete for customers, _____ is seen as a key differentiator and increasingly has become a key element of business strategy.

a. Supplier diversity
b. Customer base
c. Psychological pricing
d. Customer satisfaction

38. _____ is one of the four elements of marketing mix. An organization or set of organizations (go-betweens) involved in the process of making a product or service available for use or consumption by a consumer or business user.

The other three parts of the marketing mix are product, pricing, and promotion.

a. Better Living Through Chemistry
b. Comparison-Shopping agent
c. Japan Advertising Photographers' Association
d. Distribution

39. Mystery shopping or Mystery Consumer is a tool used by market research companies to measure quality of retail service or gather specific information about products and services. _____ posing as normal customers perform specific tasks-- such as purchasing a product, asking questions, registering complaints or behaving in a certain way - and then provide detailed reports or feedback about their experiences.

Mystery shopping began in the 1940s as a way to measure employee integrity.

a. Mystery shoppers
b. Questionnaire
c. Market research
d. Mystery shopping

40. _____ is an advertisement in which a particular product specifically mentions a competitor by name for the express purpose of showing why the competitor is inferior to the product naming it.

This should not be confused with parody advertisements, where a fictional product is being advertised for the purpose of poking fun at the particular advertisement, nor should it be confused with the use of a coined brand name for the purpose of comparing the product without actually naming an actual competitor. ('Wikipedia tastes better and is less filling than the Encyclopedia Galactica.')

In the 1980s, during what has been referred to as the cola wars, soft-drink manufacturer Pepsi ran a series of advertisements where people, caught on hidden camera, in a blind taste test, chose Pepsi over rival Coca-Cola.

a. Heavy-up
b. GL-70
c. Cost per conversion
d. Comparative advertising

Chapter 1. Marketing Research for Managerial Decision Making

41. In accounting, _____ has a very specific meaning. It is an outflow of cash or other valuable assets from a person or company to another person or company. This outflow of cash is generally one side of a trade for products or services that have equal or better current or future value to the buyer than to the seller.
   a. AMAX
   b. ADTECH
   c. ACNielsen
   d. Expense

42. _____ is a term used by project managers and project management (PM) organizations to describe methods for analyzing and collectively managing a group of current or proposed projects based on numerous key characteristics. The fundamental objective of the _____ process is to determine the optimal mix and sequencing of proposed projects to best achieve the organization's overall goals - typically expressed in terms of hard economic measures, business strategy goals, or technical strategy goals - while honoring constraints imposed by management or external real-world factors. Typical attributes of projects being analyzed in a _____ process include each project's total expected cost, consumption of scarce resources (human or otherwise) expected timeline and schedule of investment, expected nature, magnitude and timing of benefits to be realized, and relationship or inter-dependencies with other projects in the portfolio.
   a. Project Portfolio Management
   b. Pop-up ads
   c. Power III
   d. Customer intelligence

43. In economics, _____ is the desire to own something and the ability to pay for it. The term _____ signifies the ability or the willingness to buy a particular commodity at a given point of time.

   a. Market system
   b. Discretionary spending
   c. Market dominance
   d. Demand

44. _____ is a type of research conducted because a problem has not been clearly defined. _____ helps determine the best research design, data collection method and selection of subjects. Given its fundamental nature, _____ often concludes that a perceived problem does not actually exist.
   a. Exploratory research
   b. ACNielsen
   c. Intent scale translation
   d. IDDEA

45. _____ is one of the four Ps of the marketing mix. The other three aspects are product, promotion, and place. It is also a key variable in microeconomic price allocation theory.
   a. Price
   b. Relationship based pricing
   c. Pricing
   d. Competitor indexing

46. _____ is a field of inquiry that crosscuts disciplines and subject matters. _____ers aim to gather an in-depth understanding of human behavior and the reasons that govern such behavior. The discipline investigates the why and how of decision making, not just what, where, when.
   a. Qualitative research
   b. Power III
   c. 6-3-5 Brainwriting
   d. 180SearchAssistant

47. A _____ attribute is one that exists in a range of magnitudes, and can therefore be measured. Measurements of any particular _____ property are expressed as a specific quantity, referred to as a unit, multiplied by a number. Examples of physical quantities are distance, mass, and time.

a. Lifestyle city
c. BeyondROI
b. Dolly Dimples
d. Quantitative

48. _____ is a computer program used for statistical analysis.

_____ (originally, Statistical Package for the Social Sciences) was released in its first version in 1968 after being founded by Norman Nie and C. Hadlai Hull. Nie was then a political science postgraduate at Stanford University, and now Research Professor in the Department of Political Science at Stanford and Professor Emeritus of Political Science at the University of Chicago.

a. 180SearchAssistant
c. 6-3-5 Brainwriting
b. SPSS
d. Power III

49. In economics, and cost accounting, _____ describes the total economic cost of production and is made up of variable costs, which vary according to the quantity of a good produced and include inputs such as labor and raw materials, plus fixed costs, which are independent of the quantity of a good produced and include inputs (capital) that cannot be varied in the short term, such as buildings and machinery. _____ in economics includes the total opportunity cost of each factor of production in addition to fixed and variable costs.

The rate at which _____ changes as the amount produced changes is called marginal cost.

a. Total cost
c. Hoarding
b. Product proliferation
d. Household production function

50. In economics, business, retail, and accounting, a _____ is the value of money that has been used up to produce something, and hence is not available for use anymore. In economics, a _____ is an alternative that is given up as a result of a decision. In business, the _____ may be one of acquisition, in which case the amount of money expended to acquire it is counted as _____.

a. Variable cost
c. Fixed costs
b. Transaction cost
d. Cost

51. _____ is a process of gathering, modeling, and transforming data with the goal of highlighting useful information, suggesting conclusions, and supporting decision making. _____ has multiple facets and approaches, encompassing diverse techniques under a variety of names, in different business, science, and social science domains.

Data mining is a particular _____ technique that focuses on modeling and knowledge discovery for predictive rather than purely descriptive purposes.

a. 180SearchAssistant
c. 6-3-5 Brainwriting
b. Power III
d. Data analysis

52. _____ is the process of estimation in unknown situations. Prediction is a similar, but more general term. Both can refer to estimation of time series, cross-sectional or longitudinal data.

a. 180SearchAssistant
c. 6-3-5 Brainwriting
b. Power III
d. Forecasting

Chapter 1. Marketing Research for Managerial Decision Making

53. A _____ is a plan of action designed to achieve a particular goal.

_____ is different from tactics. In military terms, tactics is concerned with the conduct of an engagement while _____ is concerned with how different engagements are linked.

a. Power III
b. Strategy
c. 6-3-5 Brainwriting
d. 180SearchAssistant

54. In environmental modeling and especially in hydrology, a _____ model means a model that is acceptably consistent with observed natural processes, i.e. that simulates well, for example, observed river discharge. It is a key concept of the so-called Generalized Likelihood Uncertainty Estimation (GLUE) methodology to quantify how uncertain environmental predictions are.

a. 180SearchAssistant
b. 6-3-5 Brainwriting
c. Power III
d. Behavioral

55. Cognition is the scientific term for 'the process of thought.' Its usage varies in different ways in accord with different disciplines: For example, in psychology and _____ science it refers to an information processing view of an individual's psychological functions. Other interpretations of the meaning of cognition link it to the development of concepts; individual minds, groups, organizations, and even larger coalitions of entities, can be modelled as 'societies' (Society of Mind), which cooperate to form concepts.

The autonomous elements of each 'society' would have the opportunity to demonstrate emergent behavior in the face of some crisis or opportunity.

a. 180SearchAssistant
b. 6-3-5 Brainwriting
c. Power III
d. Cognitive

56. _____ is a form of communication that typically attempts to persuade potential customers to purchase or to consume more of a particular brand of product or service. 'While now central to the contemporary global economy and the reproduction of global production networks, it is only quite recently that _____ has been more than a marginal influence on patterns of sales and production. The formation of modern _____ was intimately bound up with the emergence of new forms of monopoly capitalism around the end of the 19th and beginning of the 20th century as one element in corporate strategies to create, organize and where possible control markets, especially for mass produced consumer goods.

a. Advertising
b. ADTECH
c. AMAX
d. ACNielsen

57. _____ , according to The American Marketing Association, is 'a planning process designed to assure that all brand contacts received by a customer or prospect for a product, service, or organization are relevant to that person and consistent over time.' (Marketing Power Dictionary)

_____ is a term used to describe a holistic approach to marketing. It aims to ensure consistency of message and the complementary use of media. The concept includes online and offline marketing channels.

a. AMAX
b. ACNielsen
c. ADTECH
d. Integrated marketing communications

Chapter 1. Marketing Research for Managerial Decision Making

58. _____ refers to messages and related media used to communicate with a market. Those who practice advertising, branding, direct marketing, graphic design, marketing, packaging, promotion, publicity, sponsorship, public relations, sales, sales promotion and online marketing are termed marketing communicators, _____ managers, or more briefly as marcom managers.
    a. Merchandise
    b. Merchandising
    c. Marketing communication
    d. Sales promotion

59. A _____ is a written document that details the necessary actions to achieve one or more marketing objectives. It can be for a product or service, a brand, or a product line. _____s cover between one and five years.
    a. Disruptive technology
    b. Marketing strategy
    c. Prosumer
    d. Marketing plan

60. _____ is a magazine, delivering news, analysis and data on marketing and media. The magazine was started as a broadsheet newspaper in Chicago in 1930. Today, its content appears in a print weekly distributed around the world and on many electronic platforms, including: AdAge.com, daily e-mail newsletters called Ad Age Daily, Ad Age's Mediaworks and Ad Age Digital; weekly newsletters such as Madison ' Vine (about branded entertainment) and Ad Age China; podcasts called Why It Matters and various videos.
    a. Outsert
    b. Advertising Age
    c. Ethical Consumer
    d. Adweek

61. Human beings are also considered to be _____ because they have the ability to change raw materials into valuable _____. The term Human _____ can also be defined as the skills, energies, talents, abilities and knowledge that are used for the production of goods or the rendering of services. While taking into account human beings as _____, the following things have to be kept in mind:

    - The size of the population
    - The capabilities of the individuals in that population

    Many _____ cannot be consumed in their original form. They have to be processed in order to change them into more usable commodities.

    a. Resources
    b. 180SearchAssistant
    c. Power III
    d. 6-3-5 Brainwriting

62. _____ is the realization of an application idea, model, design, specification, standard, algorithm an _____ is a realization of a technical specification or algorithm as a program, software component, or other computer system. Many _____s may exist for a given specification or standard.
    a. ADTECH
    b. ACNielsen
    c. AMAX
    d. Implementation

63. An _____ is the manufacturing of a good or service within a category. Although _____ is a broad term for any kind of economic production, in economics and urban planning _____ is a synonym for the secondary sector, which is a type of economic activity involved in the manufacturing of raw materials into goods and products.

There are four key industrial economic sectors: the primary sector, largely raw material extraction industries such as mining and farming; the secondary sector, involving refining, construction, and manufacturing; the tertiary sector, which deals with services (such as law and medicine) and distribution of manufactured goods; and the quaternary sector, a relatively new type of knowledge _____ focusing on technological research, design and development such as computer programming, and biochemistry.

a. AMAX
b. ACNielsen
c. Industry
d. ADTECH

64. _____ is a global marketing research firm, with worldwide headquarters in New York City. Regional headquarters for North America are located in Schaumburg, IL. As of 2008, its the part of The Nielsen Company.
a. InfoNU
b. Alloy Entertainment
c. ACNielsen
d. E-Detailing

65. _____ is a radio audience research company in the United States which collects listener data on radio audiences similar to that collected by Nielsen Media Research on television audiences. It was founded as American Research Bureau by Jim Seiler in 1949 and became bi-coastal by merging with L.A. based Coffin, Cooper and Clay in the early 1950s. ARB's initial business was the collection of television broadcast ratings exclusively.
a. Access Commerce
b. American Heart Association
c. American Cancer Society
d. Arbitron

66. In economics, an externality or spillover of an economic transaction is an impact on a party that is not directly involved in the transaction. In such a case, prices do not reflect the full costs or benefits in production or consumption of a product or service. A positive impact is called an _____ benefit, while a negative impact is called an _____ cost.
a. External
b. ADTECH
c. AMAX
d. ACNielsen

67. _____ is a property of a test intended to measure something. The test is said to have _____ if it 'looks like' it is going to measure what it is supposed to measure. For instance, if you prepare a test to measure whether students can perform multiplication, and the people you show it to all agree that it looks like a good test of multiplication ability, you have shown the _____ of your test.
a. Selective distortion
b. Power III
c. Face validity
d. 180SearchAssistant

68. _____ often refers to either primary or secondary research. Secondary research involves a company using information compiled from various sources, which is about a new or existing product. The advantages of secondary research are that it is relatively cheap and easily accessible.
a. Market Research
b. Mystery shoppers
c. Questionnaire
d. Mystery shopping

Chapter 1. Marketing Research for Managerial Decision Making   15

69. Procter is a surname, and may also refer to:

- Bryan Waller Procter (pseud. Barry Cornwall), English poet
- Goodwin Procter, American law firm
- _____, consumer products multinational

   a. Flyer   b. Convergent
   c. Black PRies   d. Procter ' Gamble

70. A _____ is a party that mediates between a buyer and a seller. A _____ who also acts as a seller or as a buyer becomes a principal party to the deal. Distinguish agent: one who acts on behalf of a principal.

   a. Broker   b. Power III
   c. 180SearchAssistant   d. Spokesperson

71. _____ is a measure of the strength of a brand, product, service relative to competitive offerings. There is often a geographic element to the competitive landscape. In defining _____, you must see to what extent a product, brand, or firm controls a product category in a given geographic area.

   a. Market system   b. Productivity
   c. Discretionary spending   d. Market dominance

72. A supply chain is the system of organizations, people, technology, activities, information and resources involved in moving a product or service from _____ to customer. Supply chain activities transform natural resources, raw materials and components into a finished product that is delivered to the end customer. In sophisticated supply chain systems, used products may re-enter the supply chain at any point where residual value is recyclable.

   a. Bringin' Home the Oil   b. Product line extension
   c. Rebate   d. Supplier

73. Founded in 1957, the _____ is one of the largest trade associations of market research and polling professionals. _____ has more than 3,000 members worldwide, representing all segments of the research industry. _____ advances, protects and promotes knowledge, standards, excellence, ethics, professional development and innovation for the global market and opinion research profession.

   a. 180SearchAssistant   b. PRSA
   c. Power III   d. Marketing Research Association

74. _____ is either an activity of a living being (such as a human), consisting of receiving knowledge of the outside world through the senses, or the recording of data using scientific instruments. The term may also refer to any datum collected during this activity.

The scientific method requires _____s of nature to formulate and test hypotheses.

   a. Observation   b. ACNielsen
   c. ADTECH   d. AMAX

75. In calculus, a function f defined on a subset of the real numbers with real values is called _____, if for all x and y such that x ≤ y one has f(x) ≤ f(y), so f preserves the order. In layman's terms, the sign of the slope is always positive (the curve tending upwards) or zero (i.e., non-decreasing, or asymptotic, or depicted as a horizontal, flat line) Likewise, a function is called monotonically decreasing (non-increasing) if, whenever x ≤ y, then f(x) ≥ f(y), so it reverses the order.
   a. Power III
   b. 180SearchAssistant
   c. 6-3-5 Brainwriting
   d. Monotonic

76. In probability theory and statistics, _____ indicates the strength and direction of a linear relationship between two random variables. That is in contrast with the usage of the term in colloquial speech, denoting any relationship, not necessarily linear. In general statistical usage, _____ or co-relation refers to the departure of two random variables from independence.
   a. Correlation
   b. Frequency distribution
   c. Probability
   d. Mean

77. _____s are used in open sentences. For instance, in the formula x + 1 = 5, x is a _____ which represents an 'unknown' number. _____s are often represented by letters of the Roman alphabet, or those of other alphabets, such as Greek, and use other special symbols.
   a. Book of business
   b. Quantitative
   c. Variable
   d. Personalization

78. The _____ and the null hypothesis are the two rival hypotheses whose likelihoods are compared by a statistical hypothesis test. Usually the _____ is the possibility that an observed effect is genuine and the null hypothesis is the rival possibility that it has resulted from chance.

The classical (or frequentist) approach is to calculate the probability that the observed effect (or one more extreme) will occur if the null hypothesis is true.

   a. Interval estimation
   b. ACNielsen
   c. Analysis of variance
   d. Alternative hypothesis

79. In statistics, _____ is a collection of statistical models, and their associated procedures, in which the observed variance is partitioned into components due to different explanatory variables. The initial techniques of the _____ were developed by the statistician and geneticist R. A. Fisher in the 1920s and 1930s, and is sometimes known as Fisher's ANOVA or Fisher's _____, due to the use of Fisher's F-distribution as part of the test of statistical significance.

There are three conceptual classes of such models:

1. Fixed-effects models assumes that the data came from normal populations which may differ only in their means. (Model 1)
2. Random effects models assume that the data describe a hierarchy of different populations whose differences are constrained by the hierarchy. (Model 2)
3. Mixed-effect models describe situations where both fixed and random effects are present. (Model 3)

Chapter 1. Marketing Research for Managerial Decision Making

In practice, there are several types of ANOVA depending on the number of treatments and the way they are applied to the subjects in the experiment:

- One-way ANOVA is used to test for differences among two or more independent groups. Typically, however, the One-way ANOVA is used to test for differences among at least three groups, since the two-group case can be covered by a T-test (Gossett, 1908.)

a. ACNielsen
b. Analysis of variance
c. Arithmetic mean
d. Interval estimation

80. In probability theory and statistics, the _____ of a random variable, probability distribution, or sample is a measure of statistical dispersion, averaging the squared distance of its possible values from the expected value (mean.) Whereas the mean is a way to describe the location of a distribution, the _____ is a way to capture its scale or degree of being spread out. The unit of _____ is the square of the unit of the original variable.

a. Correlation
b. Standard deviation
c. Sample size
d. Variance

81. In statistics, the _____ is a common measure of the correlation (linear dependence) between two variables X and Y. It is very widely used in the sciences as a measure of the strength of linear dependence between two variables, giving a value somewhere between +1 and -1 inclusive. It was first introduced by Francis Galton in the 1880s, and named after Karl Pearson.

In accordance with the usual convention, when calculated for an entire population, the Pearson product-moment correlation is typically designated by the analogous Greek letter, which in this case is ρ.

a. Standard deviation
b. Pearson product-moment correlation coefficient
c. Control chart
d. Median

82. In statistics, _____ has two related meanings:

- the arithmetic _____
- the expected value of a random variable, which is also called the population _____.

It is sometimes stated that the '_____' _____s average. This is incorrect if '_____' is taken in the specific sense of 'arithmetic _____' as there are different types of averages: the _____, median, and mode. For instance, average house prices almost always use the median value for the average. These three types of averages are all measures of locations.

a. Standard normal distribution
b. Heteroskedastic
c. Confidence interval
d. Mean

83. In statistics, _____ is a collective name for techniques for the modeling and analysis of numerical data consisting of values of a dependent variable and of one or more independent variables The dependent variable in the regression equation is modeled as a function of the independent variables, corresponding parameters, and an error term. The error term is treated as a random variable.

a. Variance inflation factor
c. Stepwise regression
b. Regression analysis
d. Multicollinearity

84. '_____' is a class of statistical techniques that can be applied to data that exhibit 'natural' groupings. _____ sorts through the raw data and groups them into clusters. A cluster is a group of relatively homogeneous cases or observations.
   a. Power III
   c. 180SearchAssistant
   b. Structure mining
   d. Cluster analysis

85. In algebra, the _____ of a polynomial with real or complex coefficients is a certain expression in the coefficients of the polynomial which is equal to zero if and only if the polynomial has a multiple root (i.e. a root with multiplicity greater than one) in the complex numbers. For example, the _____ of the quadratic polynomial

$$ax^2 + bx + c \text{ is } b^2 - 4ac.$$

The _____ of the cubic polynomial

$$ax^3 + bx^2 + cx + d \text{ is } b^2c^2 - 4ac^3 - 4b^3d - 27a^2d^2 + 18abcd.$$

   a. Lifestyle center
   c. Flighting
   b. Consumption Map
   d. Discriminant

86. Linear _____ and the related Fisher's linear discriminant are methods used in statistics and machine learning to find the linear combination of features which best separate two or more classes of objects or events. The resulting combination may be used as a linear classifier, or, more commonly, for dimensionality reduction before later classification.

LDiscriminant analysis is closely related to ANOVA (analysis of variance) and regression analysis, which also attempt to express one dependent variable as a linear combination of other features or measurements.

   a. Linear discriminant analysis
   c. Multiple discriminant analysis
   b. Discriminant analysis
   d. Geodemographic segmentation

87. _____ is a statistical method used to describe variability among observed variables in terms of fewer unobserved variables called factors. The observed variables are modeled as linear combinations of the factors, plus 'error' terms. The information gained about the interdependencies can be used later to reduce the set of variables in a dataset.
   a. Semantic differential
   c. Power III
   b. Likert scale
   d. Factor analysis

88. _____ is a statistical phenomenon in which two or more predictor variables in a multiple regression model are highly correlated. In this situation the coefficient estimates may change erratically in response to small changes in the model or the data. _____ does not reduce the predictive power or reliability of the model as a whole; it only affects calculations regarding individual predictors.
   a. Variance inflation factor
   c. Regression analysis
   b. Multicollinearity
   d. Stepwise regression

89. In statistics, _____ is used for two things;

- to construct a simple formula that will predict what value will occur for a quantity of interest when other related variables take given values.
- to allow a test to be made of whether a given variable does have an effect on a quantity of interest in situations where there may be many related variables.

In both cases, several sets of outcomes are available for the quantity of interest together with the related variables.

_____ is a form of regression analysis in which the relationship between one or more independent variables and another variable, called the dependent variable, is modelled by a least squares function, called a _____ equation. This function is a linear combination of one or more model parameters, called regression coefficients. A _____ equation with one independent variable represents a straight line when the predicted value (i.e. the dependant variable from the regression equation) is plotted against the independent variable: this is called a simple _____.

a. Heteroskedastic
b. Descriptive statistics
c. Linear regression
d. Sample size

90. An example of a repeated measures _____ would be if one group were pre- and post-tested. (This example occurs in education quite frequently.) If a teacher wanted to examine the effect of a new set of textbooks on student achievement, (s)he could test the class at the beginning of the year (pretest) and at the end of the year (posttest.)

a. T-test
b. Moving average
c. Null hypothesis
d. Statistically significant

91. In descriptive statistics, the _____ is the length of the smallest interval which contains all the data. It is calculated by subtracting the smallest observation (sample minimum) from the greatest (sample maximum) and provides an indication of statistical dispersion.

It is measured in the same units as the data.

a. Japan Advertising Photographers' Association
b. Just-In-Case
c. Personalization
d. Range

Chapter 2. The Marketing Research Process

1. _____ is defined by the American _____ Association as the activity, set of institutions, and processes for creating, communicating, delivering, and exchanging offerings that have value for customers, clients, partners, and society at large. The term developed from the original meaning which referred literally to going to market, as in shopping, or going to a market to sell goods or services.

_____ practice tends to be seen as a creative industry, which includes advertising, distribution and selling.

   a. Marketing
   b. Product naming
   c. Customer acquisition management
   d. Marketing myopia

2. Consumer market research is a form of applied sociology that concentrates on understanding the behaviours, whims and preferences, of consumers in a market-based economy, and aims to understand the effects and comparative success of marketing campaigns. The field of consumer _____ as a statistical science was pioneered by Arthur Nielsen with the founding of the ACNielsen Company in 1923 .

Thus _____ is the systematic and objective identification, collection, analysis, and dissemination of information for the purpose of assisting management in decision making related to the identification and solution of problems and opportunities in marketing.

   a. Logit analysis
   b. Focus group
   c. Marketing research process
   d. Marketing research

3. _____ is a set of six steps which defines the tasks to be accomplished in conducting a marketing research study. These include problem definition, developing an approach to problem, research design formulation, field work, data preparation and analysis, and report generation and presentation.
   a. Marketing research process
   b. Preference-rank translation
   c. Simple random sampling
   d. Market analysis

4. _____ refer to a collection of facts usually collected as the result of experience, observation or experiment or a set of premises. This may consist of numbers, words particularly as measurements or observations of a set of variables. _____ are often viewed as a lowest level of abstraction from which information and knowledge are derived.
   a. Pearson product-moment correlation coefficient
   b. Data
   c. Mean
   d. Sample size

5. A _____ is a structured collection of records or data that is stored in a computer system. The structure is achieved by organizing the data according to a _____ model. The model in most common use today is the relational model.
   a. Power III
   b. Database
   c. 6-3-5 Brainwriting
   d. 180SearchAssistant

6. _____ is a branch of philosophy which seeks to address questions about morality, such as how a moral outcome can be achieved in a specific situation (applied _____), how moral values should be determined (normative _____), what moral values people actually abide by (descriptive _____), what the fundamental semantic, ontological, and epistemic nature of _____ or morality is (meta-_____), and how moral capacity or moral agency develops and what its nature is (moral psychology.)

Chapter 2. The Marketing Research Process

Socrates was one of the first Greek philosophers to encourage both scholars and the common citizen to turn their attention from the outside world to the condition of man. In this view, Knowledge having a bearing on human life was placed highest, all other knowledge being secondary.

    a. ADTECH   b. ACNielsen
    c. AMAX   d. Ethics

7. _____ is a term for unprocessed data, it is also known as primary data. It is a relative term _____ can be input to a computer program or used in manual analysis procedures such as gathering statistics from a survey.
    a. Shoppers Food ' Pharmacy   b. Chief marketing officer
    c. Product manager   d. Raw data

8. _____ is the ability of an individual or group to seclude themselves or information about themselves and thereby reveal themselves selectively. The boundaries and content of what is considered private differ among cultures and individuals, but share basic common themes. _____ is sometimes related to anonymity, the wish to remain unnoticed or unidentified in the public realm.
    a. Privacy   b. Power III
    c. 180SearchAssistant   d. 6-3-5 Brainwriting

9. Combining Existing _____ Sources with New Primary Data Sources

Imagine that we could get hold of a good collection of surveys taken in earlier years, such as detailed studies about changes going on in this phase and hopefully additional studies in the years to come. Analyzing this data base over time could give us a good picture of what changes actually have taken place in the orientation of the population and of the extent to which new technical concepts did have an impact on subgroups of the population. Furthermore, data archives can help to prepare studies on change over time by monitoring what questions have been asked in earlier years and alerting principal investigators to important questions which should be repeated in planned research projects.

    a. Power III   b. 6-3-5 Brainwriting
    c. 180SearchAssistant   d. Secondary data

10. _____ is either an activity of a living being (such as a human), consisting of receiving knowledge of the outside world through the senses, or the recording of data using scientific instruments. The term may also refer to any datum collected during this activity.

The scientific method requires _____s of nature to formulate and test hypotheses.

    a. ADTECH   b. AMAX
    c. ACNielsen   d. Observation

11. A personal and cultural _____ is a relative ethic _____, an assumption upon which implementation can be extrapolated. A _____ system is a set of consistent _____s and measures that is soo not true. A principle _____ is a foundation upon which other _____s and measures of integrity are based.

Chapter 2. The Marketing Research Process

a. Perceptual maps
b. Package-on-Package
c. Supreme Court of the United States
d. Value

12. _____ is a rivalry between individuals, groups, nations for territory, a niche, or allocation of resources. It arises whenever two or more parties strive for a goal which cannot be shared. _____ occurs naturally between living organisms which co-exist in the same environment.

a. Non-price competition
b. Price competition
c. Price fixing
d. Competition

13. _____ in its literal sense is the process of transformation of local or regional phenomena into global ones. It can be described as a process by which the people of the world are unified into a single society and function together.

This process is a combination of economic, technological, sociocultural and political forces.

a. Power III
b. Globalization
c. 6-3-5 Brainwriting
d. 180SearchAssistant

14. A number of different _____s are indicated below.

- Randomized controlled trial
    - Double-blind randomized trial
    - Single-blind randomized trial
    - Non-blind trial
- Nonrandomized trial (quasi-experiment)
    - Interrupted time series design (measures on a sample or a series of samples from the same population are obtained several times before and after a manipulated event or a naturally occurring event) - considered a type of quasi-experiment

- Cohort study
    - Prospective cohort
    - Retrospective cohort
    - Time series study
- Case-control study
    - Nested case-control study
- Cross-sectional study
    - Community survey (a type of cross-sectional study)

When choosing a _____, many factors must be taken into account. Different types of studies are subject to different types of bias. For example, recall bias is likely to occur in cross-sectional or case-control studies where subjects are asked to recall exposure to risk factors.

a. Study design
b. 180SearchAssistant
c. Longitudinal studies
d. Power III

Chapter 2. The Marketing Research Process

15. In economics, business, retail, and accounting, a _____ is the value of money that has been used up to produce something, and hence is not available for use anymore. In economics, a _____ is an alternative that is given up as a result of a decision. In business, the _____ may be one of acquisition, in which case the amount of money expended to acquire it is counted as _____.
   a. Fixed costs
   b. Transaction cost
   c. Variable cost
   d. Cost

16. _____ is a process of gathering, modeling, and transforming data with the goal of highlighting useful information, suggesting conclusions, and supporting decision making. _____ has multiple facets and approaches, encompassing diverse techniques under a variety of names, in different business, science, and social science domains.

    Data mining is a particular _____ technique that focuses on modeling and knowledge discovery for predictive rather than purely descriptive purposes.

   a. Power III
   b. 180SearchAssistant
   c. 6-3-5 Brainwriting
   d. Data analysis

17. _____ is the process of extracting hidden patterns from data. As more data is gathered, with the amount of data doubling every three years, _____ is becoming an increasingly important tool to transform this data into information. It is commonly used in a wide range of profiling practices, such as marketing, surveillance, fraud detection and scientific discovery.
   a. Power III
   b. 180SearchAssistant
   c. Data mining
   d. Structure mining

18. _____s are used in open sentences. For instance, in the formula x + 1 = 5, x is a _____ which represents an 'unknown' number. _____s are often represented by letters of the Roman alphabet, or those of other alphabets, such as Greek, and use other special symbols.
   a. Book of business
   b. Personalization
   c. Quantitative
   d. Variable

19. _____ is a computer program used for statistical analysis.

    _____ (originally, Statistical Package for the Social Sciences) was released in its first version in 1968 after being founded by Norman Nie and C. Hadlai Hull. Nie was then a political science postgraduate at Stanford University, and now Research Professor in the Department of Political Science at Stanford and Professor Emeritus of Political Science at the University of Chicago.

   a. Power III
   b. 180SearchAssistant
   c. 6-3-5 Brainwriting
   d. SPSS

20. _____ consists of the processes a company uses to track and organize its contacts with its current and prospective customers. _____ software is used to support these processes; information about customers and customer interactions can be entered, stored and accessed by employees in different company departments. Typical _____ goals are to improve services provided to customers, and to use customer contact information for targeted marketing.

a. Product bundling
b. Commercialization
c. Customer relationship management
d. Demand generation

21. _____ is a term used to describe a process of preparing and collecting data - for example as part of a process improvement or similar project.

_____ usually takes place early on in an improvement project, and is often formalised through a _____ Plan which often contains the following activity.

1. Pre collection activity - Agree goals, target data, definitions, methods
2. Collection - _____
3. Present Findings - usually involves some form of sorting analysis and/or presentation.

A formal _____ process is necessary as it ensures that data gathered is both defined and accurate and that subsequent decisions based on arguments embodied in the findings are valid . The process provides both a baseline from which to measure from and in certain cases a target on what to improve. Types of _____ 1-By mail questionnaires 2-By personal interview

- Six sigma
- Sampling (statistics)

a. 180SearchAssistant
b. Power III
c. 6-3-5 Brainwriting
d. Data collection

22. A _____ is a research instrument consisting of a series of questions and other prompts for the purpose of gathering information from respondents. Although they are often designed for statistical analysis of the responses, this is not always the case. The _____ was invented by Sir Francis Galton.
a. Market research
b. Mystery shopping
c. Mystery shoppers
d. Questionnaire

23. _____ is that part of statistical practice concerned with the selection of individual observations intended to yield some knowledge about a population of concern, especially for the purposes of statistical inference. Each observation measures one or more properties (weight, location, etc.) of an observable entity enumerated to distinguish objects or individuals.
a. Sampling
b. Richard Buckminster 'Bucky' Fuller
c. AStore
d. Sports Marketing Group

24. _____ is a marketing term, and involves evaluating the situation and trends in a particular company's market. _____ is often called the 'three c's', which refers to the three major elements that must be studied:

- Customers
- Costs
- Competition

The number of 'c's' is sometimes extended to four, five, or even six, with 'Collaboration', 'Company', and 'Competitive advantage'.

- Marketing mix
- SWOT analysis

a. Power III
c. 6-3-5 Brainwriting
b. Situation analysis
d. 180SearchAssistant

25. _____ a research method involving the use of questionnaires and/or statistical surveys to gather data about people and their thoughts and behaviours.
   a. T-test
   c. Z-test
   b. Control chart
   d. Survey research

26. Customer _____ consists of the processes a company uses to track and organize its contacts with its current and prospective customers. CRelationship management software is used to support these processes; information about customers and customer interactions can be entered, stored and accessed by employees in different company departments. Typical CRelationship management goals are to improve services provided to customers, and to use customer contact information for targeted marketing.
   a. Product bundling
   c. Green marketing
   b. Marketing
   d. Relationship management

27. The _____ is the major entity that is being analyzed in the study. It is the 'what' or 'whom' that is being studied. In social science research, the most typical units of analysis are individual people.
   a. AMAX
   c. ADTECH
   b. ACNielsen
   d. Unit of analysis

28. A _____ is a commercial building for storage of goods. _____s are used by manufacturers, importers, exporters, wholesalers, transport businesses, customs, etc. They are usually large plain buildings in industrial areas of cities and towns.
   a. Warehouse
   c. Power III
   b. 6-3-5 Brainwriting
   d. 180SearchAssistant

29. _____, a business term, is a measure of how products and services supplied by a company meet or surpass customer expectation. It is seen as a key performance indicator within business and is part of the four perspectives of a Balanced Scorecard.

In a competitive marketplace where businesses compete for customers, _____ is seen as a key differentiator and increasingly has become a key element of business strategy.

   a. Supplier diversity
   c. Customer base
   b. Customer satisfaction
   d. Psychological pricing

Chapter 2. The Marketing Research Process

30. _____ describes data and characteristics about the population or phenomenon being studied. _____ answers the questions who, what, where, when and how.

Although the data description is factual, accurate and systematic, the research cannot describe what caused a situation.

- a. Two-tailed test
- c. Sampling error
- b. Power III
- d. Descriptive research

31. _____ is a type of research conducted because a problem has not been clearly defined. _____ helps determine the best research design, data collection method and selection of subjects. Given its fundamental nature, _____ often concludes that a perceived problem does not actually exist.
- a. IDDEA
- c. Exploratory research
- b. Intent scale translation
- d. ACNielsen

32. _____ is a field of inquiry that crosscuts disciplines and subject matters . _____ers aim to gather an in-depth understanding of human behavior and the reasons that govern such behavior. The discipline investigates the why and how of decision making, not just what, where, when.
- a. 180SearchAssistant
- c. Power III
- b. 6-3-5 Brainwriting
- d. Qualitative research

33. _____ is the provision of service to customers before, during and after a purchase.

According to Turban et al., '_____ is a series of activities designed to enhance the level of customer satisfaction - that is, the feeling that a product or service has met the customer expectation.'

Its importance varies by product, industry and customer.

- a. Customer service
- c. Facing
- b. Customer experience
- d. COPC Inc.

34. _____ is an advertisement in which a particular product specifically mentions a competitor by name for the express purpose of showing why the competitor is inferior to the product naming it.

This should not be confused with parody advertisements, where a fictional product is being advertised for the purpose of poking fun at the particular advertisement, nor should it be confused with the use of a coined brand name for the purpose of comparing the product without actually naming an actual competitor. ('Wikipedia tastes better and is less filling than the Encyclopedia Galactica.')

In the 1980s, during what has been referred to as the cola wars, soft-drink manufacturer Pepsi ran a series of advertisements where people, caught on hidden camera, in a blind taste test, chose Pepsi over rival Coca-Cola.

- a. Comparative advertising
- c. Heavy-up
- b. Cost per conversion
- d. GL-70

Chapter 2. The Marketing Research Process

35. A _____ is a form of qualitative research in which a group of people are asked about their attitude towards a product, service, concept, advertisement, idea, or packaging. Questions are asked in an interactive group setting where participants are free to talk with other group members.

Ernest Dichter originated the idea of having a 'group therapy' for products and this process is what became known as a _____.

   a. Cross tabulation   b. Focus group
   c. Logit analysis   d. Marketing research process

36. The _____ of a statistical sample is the number of observations that constitute it. It is typically denoted n, a positive integer (natural number.)

Typically, all else being equal, a larger _____ leads to increased precision in estimates of various properties of the population.

   a. Heteroskedastic   b. Data
   c. Frequency distribution   d. Sample size

37. Sampling is the use of a subset of the population to represent the whole population. Probability sampling, or random sampling, is a sampling technique in which the probability of getting any particular sample may be calculated. _____ does not meet this criterion and should be used with caution.

   a. Snowball sampling   b. Power III
   c. Quota sampling   d. Nonprobability sampling

38. _____ is a way of expressing knowledge or belief that an event will occur or has occurred. In mathematics the concept has been given an exact meaning in _____ theory, that is used extensively in such areas of study as mathematics, statistics, finance, gambling, science, and philosophy to draw conclusions about the likelihood of potential events and the underlying mechanics of complex systems.

   a. Data   b. Probability
   c. Heteroskedastic   d. Linear regression

39. In statistics, _____ or estimation error is the error caused by observing a sample instead of the whole population.

An estimate of a quantity of interest, such as an average or percentage, will generally be subject to sample-to-sample variation. These variations in the possible sample values of a statistic can theoretically be expressed as _____s, although in practice the exact _____ is typically unknown.

   a. Sampling error   b. Two-tailed test
   c. Power III   d. Varimax rotation

40. _____ is a sampling technique used when 'natural' groupings are evident in a statistical population. It is often used in marketing research. In this technique, the total population is divided into these groups (or clusters) and a sample of the groups is selected.

a. Snowball sampling
b. Quota sampling
c. Power III
d. Cluster sampling

41. In statistics, a _____ is an interval estimate of a population parameter. Instead of estimating the parameter by a single value, an interval likely to include the parameter is given. Thus, _____s are used to indicate the reliability of an estimate.
   a. Sample mean
   b. Linear regression
   c. T-test
   d. Confidence interval

42. _____ is anything that is intended to save time, energy or frustration. A _____ store at a petrol station, for example, sells items that have nothing to do with gasoline/petrol, but it saves the consumer from having to go to a grocery store. '_____' is a very relative term and its meaning tends to change over time.
   a. Demographic profile
   b. MaxDiff
   c. Marketing buzz
   d. Convenience

43. _____ is a type of nonprobability sampling which involves the sample being drawn from that part of the population which is close to hand. That is, a sample population selected because it is readily available and convenient. The researcher using such a sample cannot scientifically make generalizations about the total population from this sample because it would not be representative enough.
   a. ADTECH
   b. ACNielsen
   c. Accidental sampling
   d. AMAX

44. The _____ and the null hypothesis are the two rival hypotheses whose likelihoods are compared by a statistical hypothesis test. Usually the _____ is the possibility that an observed effect is genuine and the null hypothesis is the rival possibility that it has resulted from chance.

The classical (or frequentist) approach is to calculate the probability that the observed effect (or one more extreme) will occur if the null hypothesis is true.

   a. Alternative hypothesis
   b. ACNielsen
   c. Interval estimation
   d. Analysis of variance

45. _____ is a form of communication that typically attempts to persuade potential customers to purchase or to consume more of a particular brand of product or service. 'While now central to the contemporary global economy and the reproduction of global production networks, it is only quite recently that _____ has been more than a marginal influence on patterns of sales and production. The formation of modern _____ was intimately bound up with the emergence of new forms of monopoly capitalism around the end of the 19th and beginning of the 20th century as one element in corporate strategies to create, organize and where possible control markets, especially for mass produced consumer goods.
   a. ACNielsen
   b. AMAX
   c. ADTECH
   d. Advertising

46. In statistics, the _____ is a common measure of the correlation (linear dependence) between two variables X and Y. It is very widely used in the sciences as a measure of the strength of linear dependence between two variables, giving a value somewhere between +1 and -1 inclusive. It was first introduced by Francis Galton in the 1880s, and named after Karl Pearson.

In accordance with the usual convention, when calculated for an entire population, the Pearson product-moment correlation is typically designated by the analogous Greek letter, which in this case is ρ .

a. Control chart
c. Median
b. Standard deviation
d. Pearson product-moment correlation coefficient

47. In probability theory and statistics, _____ indicates the strength and direction of a linear relationship between two random variables. That is in contrast with the usage of the term in colloquial speech, denoting any relationship, not necessarily linear. In general statistical usage, _____ or co-relation refers to the departure of two random variables from independence.

a. Probability
c. Correlation
b. Mean
d. Frequency distribution

Chapter 3. Information Management for Marketing Decisions: Secondary Data Sources

1. Combining Existing _____ Sources with New Primary Data Sources

Imagine that we could get hold of a good collection of surveys taken in earlier years, such as detailed studies about changes going on in this phase and hopefully additional studies in the years to come. Analyzing this data base over time could give us a good picture of what changes actually have taken place in the orientation of the population and of the extent to which new technical concepts did have an impact on subgroups of the population. Furthermore, data archives can help to prepare studies on change over time by monitoring what questions have been asked in earlier years and alerting principal investigators to important questions which should be repeated in planned research projects.

 a. Power III
 b. 180SearchAssistant
 c. 6-3-5 Brainwriting
 d. Secondary data

2. _____ refer to a collection of facts usually collected as the result of experience, observation or experiment or a set of premises. This may consist of numbers, words particularly as measurements or observations of a set of variables. _____ are often viewed as a lowest level of abstraction from which information and knowledge are derived.

 a. Sample size
 b. Pearson product-moment correlation coefficient
 c. Mean
 d. Data

3. _____ consists of the processes a company uses to track and organize its contacts with its current and prospective customers. _____ software is used to support these processes; information about customers and customer interactions can be entered, stored and accessed by employees in different company departments. Typical _____ goals are to improve services provided to customers, and to use customer contact information for targeted marketing.

 a. Product bundling
 b. Demand generation
 c. Customer relationship management
 d. Commercialization

4. A _____ is a structured collection of records or data that is stored in a computer system. The structure is achieved by organizing the data according to a _____ model. The model in most common use today is the relational model.

 a. Database
 b. Power III
 c. 180SearchAssistant
 d. 6-3-5 Brainwriting

5. _____ is defined by the American _____ Association as the activity, set of institutions, and processes for creating, communicating, delivering, and exchanging offerings that have value for customers, clients, partners, and society at large. The term developed from the original meaning which referred literally to going to market, as in shopping, or going to a market to sell goods or services.

_____ practice tends to be seen as a creative industry, which includes advertising, distribution and selling.

 a. Customer acquisition management
 b. Product naming
 c. Marketing myopia
 d. Marketing

6. Consumer market research is a form of applied sociology that concentrates on understanding the behaviours, whims and preferences, of consumers in a market-based economy, and aims to understand the effects and comparative success of marketing campaigns. The field of consumer _____ as a statistical science was pioneered by Arthur Nielsen with the founding of the ACNielsen Company in 1923.

Thus _____ is the systematic and objective identification, collection, analysis, and dissemination of information for the purpose of assisting management in decision making related to the identification and solution of problems and opportunities in marketing.

a. Logit analysis
c. Focus group
b. Marketing research process
d. Marketing Research

7. _____ is a form of marketing developed from direct response marketing campaigns conducted in the 1970's and 1980's which emphasizes customer retention and satisfaction, rather than a dominant focus on 'point of sale' transactions.

_____ differs from other forms of marketing in that it recognizes the long term value to the firm of keeping customers, as opposed to direct or 'Intrusion' marketing, which focuses upon acquisition of new clients by targeting majority demographics based upon prospective client lists.

_____ refers to long-term and mutually beneficial arrangement wherein both buyer and seller focus on value enhancement through the certain of more satisfying exchange. This approach attempts to transcend the simple purchase exchange process with customer to make more meaningful and richer contact by providing a more holistic, personalized purchase, and use orn consumption experience to create stronger ties.

a. Global marketing
c. Guerrilla Marketing
b. Diversity marketing
d. Relationship marketing

8. A _____, in the field of business and marketing, is a geographic region or demographic group used to gauge the viability of a product or service in the mass market prior to a wide scale roll-out. The criteria used to judge the acceptability of a _____ region or group include:

1. a population that is demographically similar to the proposed target market; and
2. relative isolation from densely populated media markets so that advertising to the test audience can be efficient and economical.

The _____ ideally aims to duplicate 'everything' - promotion and distribution as well as `product' - on a smaller scale. The technique replicates, typically in one area, what is planned to occur in a national launch; and the results are very carefully monitored, so that they can be extrapolated to projected national results. The `area' may be any one of the following:

- Television area
- Test town
- Residential neighborhood
- Test site

Chapter 3. Information Management for Marketing Decisions: Secondary Data Sources

A number of decisions have to be taken about any _____:

- Which _____?
- What is to be tested?
- How long a test?
- What are the success criteria?

The simple go or no-go decision, together with the related reduction of risk, is normally the main justification for the expense of _____s. At the same time, however, such _____s can be used to test specific elements of a new product's marketing mix; possibly the version of the product itself, the promotional message and media spend, the distribution channels and the price.

    a. 180SearchAssistant
    c. Test market
    b. Preadolescence
    d. Power III

9. An _____ is a special-purpose computer system designed to perform one or a few dedicated functions, often with real-time computing constraints. It is usually embedded as part of a complete device including hardware and mechanical parts. In contrast, a general-purpose computer, such as a personal computer, can do many different tasks depending on programming.
    a. AMAX
    c. Embedded system
    b. ACNielsen
    d. ADTECH

10. _____ is a type of research conducted because a problem has not been clearly defined. _____ helps determine the best research design, data collection method and selection of subjects. Given its fundamental nature, _____ often concludes that a perceived problem does not actually exist.
    a. IDDEA
    c. Intent scale translation
    b. ACNielsen
    d. Exploratory research

11. In economics, an externality or spillover of an economic transaction is an impact on a party that is not directly involved in the transaction. In such a case, prices do not reflect the full costs or benefits in production or consumption of a product or service. A positive impact is called an _____ benefit, while a negative impact is called an _____ cost.
    a. AMAX
    c. ACNielsen
    b. ADTECH
    d. External

12. Customer _____ consists of the processes a company uses to track and organize its contacts with its current and prospective customers. CRelationship management software is used to support these processes; information about customers and customer interactions can be entered, stored and accessed by employees in different company departments. Typical CRelationship management goals are to improve services provided to customers, and to use customer contact information for targeted marketing.
    a. Green marketing
    c. Marketing
    b. Product bundling
    d. Relationship management

Chapter 3. Information Management for Marketing Decisions: Secondary Data Sources

13. A number of different _____s are indicated below.

- Randomized controlled trial
    - Double-blind randomized trial
    - Single-blind randomized trial
    - Non-blind trial
- Nonrandomized trial (quasi-experiment)
    - Interrupted time series design (measures on a sample or a series of samples from the same population are obtained several times before and after a manipulated event or a naturally occurring event) - considered a type of quasi-experiment

- Cohort study
    - Prospective cohort
    - Retrospective cohort
    - Time series study
- Case-control study
    - Nested case-control study
- Cross-sectional study
    - Community survey (a type of cross-sectional study)

When choosing a _____, many factors must be taken into account. Different types of studies are subject to different types of bias. For example, recall bias is likely to occur in cross-sectional or case-control studies where subjects are asked to recall exposure to risk factors.

a. 180SearchAssistant
b. Power III
c. Longitudinal studies
d. Study design

14. A personal and cultural _____ is a relative ethic _____, an assumption upon which implementation can be extrapolated. A _____ system is a set of consistent _____s and measures that is soo not true. A principle _____ is a foundation upon which other _____s and measures of integrity are based.

a. Perceptual maps
b. Package-on-Package
c. Value
d. Supreme Court of the United States

15. _____ is a term for unprocessed data, it is also known as primary data. It is a relative term _____ can be input to a computer program or used in manual analysis procedures such as gathering statistics from a survey.

a. Chief marketing officer
b. Product manager
c. Shoppers Food ' Pharmacy
d. Raw data

16. Competitiveness is a comparative concept of the ability and performance of a firm, sub-sector or country to sell and supply goods and/or services in a given market. Although widely used in economics and business management, the usefulness of the concept, particularly in the context of national competitiveness, is vigorously disputed by economists, such as Paul Krugman .

The term may also be applied to markets, where it is used to refer to the extent to which the market structure may be regarded as perfectly _____.

a. Geographical pricing
b. Customs union
c. Free trade zone
d. Competitive

17. In economics, business, retail, and accounting, a _____ is the value of money that has been used up to produce something, and hence is not available for use anymore. In economics, a _____ is an alternative that is given up as a result of a decision. In business, the _____ may be one of acquisition, in which case the amount of money expended to acquire it is counted as _____.

a. Variable cost
b. Cost
c. Transaction cost
d. Fixed costs

18. The _____ is the group of customers and/or consumers that a business serves. In the most situations, a large part of this group is made up of repeat customers with a high ratio of purchase over time. These customers are the main source of consumer spending.

a. Psychological pricing
b. Supplier diversity
c. First-mover advantage
d. Customer base

19. _____ is the process of extracting hidden patterns from data. As more data is gathered, with the amount of data doubling every three years, _____ is becoming an increasingly important tool to transform this data into information. It is commonly used in a wide range of profiling practices, such as marketing, surveillance, fraud detection and scientific discovery.

a. 180SearchAssistant
b. Structure mining
c. Power III
d. Data mining

20. In marketing, customer _____, lifetime customer value (LCV), or _____ (LTV) and a new concept of 'customer life cycle management' is the present value of the future cash flows attributed to the customer relationship. Use of customer _____ as a marketing metric tends to place greater emphasis on customer service and long-term customer satisfaction, rather than on maximizing short-term sales.

Customer _____ has intuitive appeal as a marketing concept, because in theory it represents exactly how much each customer is worth in monetary terms, and therefore exactly how much a marketing department should be willing to spend to acquire each customer.

a. Value chain
b. Lifetime value
c. Brand infiltration
d. Sweepstakes

21. _____ is a term used to describe a process of preparing and collecting data - for example as part of a process improvement or similar project.

_____ usually takes place early on in an improvement project, and is often formalised through a _____ Plan which often contains the following activity.

1. Pre collection activity - Agree goals, target data, definitions, methods
2. Collection - _____
3. Present Findings - usually involves some form of sorting analysis and/or presentation.

Chapter 3. Information Management for Marketing Decisions: Secondary Data Sources 35

A formal _____ process is necessary as it ensures that data gathered is both defined and accurate and that subsequent decisions based on arguments embodied in the findings are valid . The process provides both a baseline from which to measure from and in certain cases a target on what to improve. Types of _____ 1-By mail questionnaires 2-By personal interview

- Six sigma
- Sampling (statistics)

.

   a. 6-3-5 Brainwriting   b. 180SearchAssistant
   c. Power III   d. Data collection

22. _____ is systematic determination of merit, worth, and significance of something or someone using criteria against a set of standards. _____ often is used to characterize and appraise subjects of interest in a wide range of human enterprises, including the arts, criminal justice, foundations and non-profit organizations, government, health care, and other human services.

Depending on the topic of interest, there are professional groups which look to the quality and rigor of the _____ process.

   a. ADTECH   b. ACNielsen
   c. AMAX   d. Evaluation

23. _____ is a standard point of view or personal prejudice. especially when the tendency interferes with the ability to be impartial, unprejudiced, or objective. The term _____ed is used to describe an action, judgment, or other outcome influenced by a prejudged perspective.
   a. Bias   b. 180SearchAssistant
   c. 6-3-5 Brainwriting   d. Power III

24. In accounting, _____ has a very specific meaning. It is an outflow of cash or other valuable assets from a person or company to another person or company. This outflow of cash is generally one side of a trade for products or services that have equal or better current or future value to the buyer than to the seller.
   a. ACNielsen   b. AMAX
   c. ADTECH   d. Expense

25. _____ in organizations and public policy is both the organizational process of creating and maintaining a plan; and the psychological process of thinking about the activities required to create a desired goal on some scale. As such, it is a fundamental property of intelligent behavior. This thought process is essential to the creation and refinement of a plan, or integration of it with other plans, that is, it combines forecasting of developments with the preparation of scenarios of how to react to them.
   a. 6-3-5 Brainwriting   b. 180SearchAssistant
   c. Planning   d. Power III

26. A _____ is a plan of action designed to achieve a particular goal.

36 *Chapter 3. Information Management for Marketing Decisions: Secondary Data Sources*

_____ is different from tactics. In military terms, tactics is concerned with the conduct of an engagement while _____ is concerned with how different engagements are linked.

a. 6-3-5 Brainwriting
c. Power III

b. Strategy
d. 180SearchAssistant

27. The United States _____ is the government agency that is responsible for the United States Census. It also gathers other national demographic and economic data.

a. 180SearchAssistant
c. 6-3-5 Brainwriting

b. Power III
d. Census Bureau

28. An _____ is the manufacturing of a good or service within a category. Although _____ is a broad term for any kind of economic production, in economics and urban planning _____ is a synonym for the secondary sector, which is a type of economic activity involved in the manufacturing of raw materials into goods and products.

There are four key industrial economic sectors: the primary sector, largely raw material extraction industries such as mining and farming; the secondary sector, involving refining, construction, and manufacturing; the tertiary sector, which deals with services (such as law and medicine) and distribution of manufactured goods; and the quaternary sector, a relatively new type of knowledge _____ focusing on technological research, design and development such as computer programming, and biochemistry.

a. ADTECH
c. AMAX

b. ACNielsen
d. Industry

29. The _____ or _____ is used by business and government to classify and measure economic activity in Canada, Mexico and the United States. It has largely replaced the older Standard Industrial Classification system; however, certain government departments and agencies, such as the U.S. Securities and Exchange Commission (SEC), still use the SIC codes.

The _____ numbering system is a six-digit code.

a. Power III
c. 180SearchAssistant

b. 6-3-5 Brainwriting
d. North American Industry Classification System

30. _____s are used in open sentences. For instance, in the formula $x + 1 = 5$, x is a _____ which represents an 'unknown' number. _____s are often represented by letters of the Roman alphabet, or those of other alphabets, such as Greek, and use other special symbols.

a. Book of business
c. Personalization

b. Variable
d. Quantitative

31. The United States _____ is the Cabinet department of the United States government concerned with promoting economic growth. It was originally created as the United States _____ and Labor on February 14, 1903. It was subsequently renamed to the _____ on March 4, 1913, and its bureaus and agencies specializing in labor were transferred to the new Department of Labor.

Chapter 3. Information Management for Marketing Decisions: Secondary Data Sources

    a. 180SearchAssistant
    b. Power III
    c. 6-3-5 Brainwriting
    d. Department of Commerce

32. The _____ is the Cabinet department of the United States government concerned with promoting economic growth. It was originally created as the _____ and Labor on February 14, 1903. It was subsequently renamed to the Department of Commerce on March 4, 1913, and its bureaus and agencies specializing in labor were transferred to the new Department of Labor.
    a. AMAX
    b. United States Department of Commerce
    c. ACNielsen
    d. ADTECH

33. _____ or _____ data refers to selected population characteristics as used in government, marketing or opinion research, or the _____ profiles used in such research. Note the distinction from the term 'demography' Commonly-used _____ include race, age, income, disabilities, mobility (in terms of travel time to work or number of vehicles available), educational attainment, home ownership, employment status, and even location.
    a. AStore
    b. Albert Einstein
    c. Demographic
    d. African Americans

34. _____s is the social science that studies the production, distribution, and consumption of goods and services. The term _____s comes from the Ancient Greek oá¼°κονομῖα from oá¼¶κος (oikos, 'house') + νόμος (nomos, 'custom' or 'law'), hence 'rules of the house(hold)'. Current _____ models developed out of the broader field of political economy in the late 19th century, owing to a desire to use an empirical approach more akin to the physical sciences.
    a. ADTECH
    b. ACNielsen
    c. Industrial organization
    d. Economic

35. A _____ is a type of wholesale merchant business that buys goods and bulk products from importers, other wholesalers and then sells to retailers. _____s can deal in any commodity destined for the retail market. Typical categories are food, lumber, hardware, fuel, and textiles.
    a. Chief privacy officer
    b. Refusal to deal
    c. Jobbing house
    d. Tacit collusion

36. _____ is the practice of individuals including commercial businesses, governments and institutions, facilitating the sale of their products or services to other companies or organizations that in turn resell them, use them as components in products or services they offer _____ is also called business-to-_____ for short. (Note that while marketing to government entities shares some of the same dynamics of organizational marketing, B2G Marketing is meaningfully different.)
    a. Disruptive technology
    b. Law of disruption
    c. Mass marketing
    d. Business marketing

37. A _____ is a documented investigation of a Market that is used to inform a firm's planning activities particularly around decision of: inventory, purchase, work force expansion/contraction, facility expansion, purchases of capital equipment, promotional activities, and many other aspects of a company.

Not all managers are asked to conduct a _____, but all managers must make decisions using _____ data and understand how the data was derived. So all managers need a reasonable understanding of the tools most used for making sales forecasts and analyzing markets.

Chapter 3. Information Management for Marketing Decisions: Secondary Data Sources

a. Market Analysis
b. Cross tabulation
c. Preference regression
d. Simple random sampling

38. _____ refers to the methods, practices and operations conducted to promote and sustain certain categories of commercial activity. The term is understood to have different specific meanings depending on the context. Merchandise is a sale goods at a store

In marketing, one of the definitions of _____ is the practice in which the brand or image from one product or service is used to sell another.

a. New Media Strategies
b. Word of mouth
c. Marketing communication
d. Merchandising

39. _____ is a mathematical science pertaining to the collection, analysis, interpretation or explanation, and presentation of data. It also provides tools for prediction and forecasting based on data. It is applicable to a wide variety of academic disciplines, from the natural and social sciences to the humanities, government and business.

a. Null hypothesis
b. Median
c. Type I error
d. Statistics

40. The _____ is an English-language international daily newspaper published by Dow Jones ' Company in New York City with Asian and European editions. As of 2007, It has a worldwide daily circulation of more than 2 million, with approximately 931,000 paying online subscribers. It was the largest-circulation newspaper in the United States until November 2003, when it was surpassed by USA Today.

a. Wall Street Journal
b. Power III
c. 6-3-5 Brainwriting
d. 180SearchAssistant

41. _____ is a broad label that refers to any individuals or households that use goods and services generated within the economy. The concept of a _____ is used in different contexts, so that the usage and significance of the term may vary.

A _____ is a person who uses any product or service.

a. Consumer
b. 6-3-5 Brainwriting
c. Power III
d. 180SearchAssistant

42. Human beings are also considered to be _____ because they have the ability to change raw materials into valuable _____. The term Human _____ can also be defined as the skills, energies, talents, abilities and knowledge that are used for the production of goods or the rendering of services. While taking into account human beings as _____, the following things have to be kept in mind:

- The size of the population
- The capabilities of the individuals in that population

Many _____ cannot be consumed in their original form. They have to be processed in order to change them into more usable commodities.

Chapter 3. Information Management for Marketing Decisions: Secondary Data Sources

a. Power III
b. 6-3-5 Brainwriting
c. Resources
d. 180SearchAssistant

43. _____ is a type of cognitive bias which can affect the results of a statistical survey if respondents answer questions in the way they think the questioner wants them to answer rather than according to their true beliefs. This may occur if the questioner is obviously angling for a particular answer (as in push polling) or if the respondent wishes to please the questioner by answering what appears to be the 'morally right' answer. An example of the latter might be if a woman surveys a man on his attitudes to domestic violence, or someone who obviously cares about the environment asks people how much they value a wilderness area.

a. Power III
b. Response bias
c. 180SearchAssistant
d. Von Restorff effect

44. _____ is that part of statistical practice concerned with the selection of individual observations intended to yield some knowledge about a population of concern, especially for the purposes of statistical inference. Each observation measures one or more properties (weight, location, etc.) of an observable entity enumerated to distinguish objects or individuals.

a. AStore
b. Richard Buckminster 'Bucky' Fuller
c. Sports Marketing Group
d. Sampling

45. In statistics, _____ or estimation error is the error caused by observing a sample instead of the whole population.

An estimate of a quantity of interest, such as an average or percentage, will generally be subject to sample-to-sample variation. These variations in the possible sample values of a statistic can theoretically be expressed as _____s, although in practice the exact _____ is typically unknown.

a. Varimax rotation
b. Power III
c. Two-tailed test
d. Sampling error

46. _____ a research method involving the use of questionnaires and/or statistical surveys to gather data about people and their thoughts and behaviours.

a. Z-test
b. Survey research
c. T-test
d. Control chart

47. In statistics, a _____ is an interval estimate of a population parameter. Instead of estimating the parameter by a single value, an interval likely to include the parameter is given. Thus, _____s are used to indicate the reliability of an estimate.

a. Sample mean
b. Linear regression
c. T-test
d. Confidence interval

48. _____ is a process of gathering, modeling, and transforming data with the goal of highlighting useful information, suggesting conclusions, and supporting decision making. _____ has multiple facets and approaches, encompassing diverse techniques under a variety of names, in different business, science, and social science domains.

Data mining is a particular _____ technique that focuses on modeling and knowledge discovery for predictive rather than purely descriptive purposes.

Chapter 3. Information Management for Marketing Decisions: Secondary Data Sources

a. Power III
b. Data analysis
c. 6-3-5 Brainwriting
d. 180SearchAssistant

49. _____ is a global marketing research firm, with worldwide headquarters in New York City. Regional headquarters for North America are located in Schaumburg, IL. As of 2008, its the part of The Nielsen Company.
a. E-Detailing
b. Alloy Entertainment
c. InfoNU
d. ACNielsen

50. _____ is a radio audience research company in the United States which collects listener data on radio audiences similar to that collected by Nielsen Media Research on television audiences. It was founded as American Research Bureau by Jim Seiler in 1949 and became bi-coastal by merging with L.A. based Coffin, Cooper and Clay in the early 1950s. ARB's initial business was the collection of television broadcast ratings exclusively.
a. American Heart Association
b. American Cancer Society
c. Access Commerce
d. Arbitron

51. _____ is an advertisement in which a particular product specifically mentions a competitor by name for the express purpose of showing why the competitor is inferior to the product naming it.

This should not be confused with parody advertisements, where a fictional product is being advertised for the purpose of poking fun at the particular advertisement, nor should it be confused with the use of a coined brand name for the purpose of comparing the product without actually naming an actual competitor. ('Wikipedia tastes better and is less filling than the Encyclopedia Galactica.')

In the 1980s, during what has been referred to as the cola wars, soft-drink manufacturer Pepsi ran a series of advertisements where people, caught on hidden camera, in a blind taste test, chose Pepsi over rival Coca-Cola.

a. Comparative advertising
b. GL-70
c. Heavy-up
d. Cost per conversion

52. _____ is a specialized field of marketing research, it is the study of television commercials prior to airing them. It is defined as research to determine an ad's effectiveness based on consumers' responses to the ad and covers all media including print, TV, radio, Internet etcAlthough also known as _____, pre-testing is considered the more accurate, modern name (Young, p.4) for the prediction of how effectively an ad will perform, based on the analysis of feedback gathered from the target audience. Each test will either qualify the ad as strong enough to meet company action standards for airing or identify opportunities to improve the performance of the ad through editing.
a. Johnson Box
b. Custom media
c. Heinz pickle pin
d. Copy Testing

53. The general definition of an _____ is an evaluation of a person, organization, system, process, project or product. _____s are performed to ascertain the validity and reliability of information; also to provide an assessment of a system's internal control. The goal of an _____ is to express an opinion on the person/organization/system (etc) in question, under evaluation based on work done on a test basis.
a. ACNielsen
b. AMAX
c. ADTECH
d. Audit

54. In statistics, the _____ is a common measure of the correlation (linear dependence) between two variables X and Y. It is very widely used in the sciences as a measure of the strength of linear dependence between two variables, giving a value somewhere between +1 and -1 inclusive. It was first introduced by Francis Galton in the 1880s, and named after Karl Pearson.

In accordance with the usual convention, when calculated for an entire population, the Pearson product-moment correlation is typically designated by the analogous Greek letter, which in this case is ρ .

    a. Median   b. Control chart
    c. Standard deviation   d. Pearson product-moment correlation coefficient

55. In probability theory and statistics, _____ indicates the strength and direction of a linear relationship between two random variables. That is in contrast with the usage of the term in colloquial speech, denoting any relationship, not necessarily linear. In general statistical usage, _____ or co-relation refers to the departure of two random variables from independence.
    a. Mean   b. Probability
    c. Frequency distribution   d. Correlation

56. Procter is a surname, and may also refer to:

- Bryan Waller Procter (pseud. Barry Cornwall), English poet
- Goodwin Procter, American law firm
- _____, consumer products multinational

    a. Procter ' Gamble   b. Flyer
    c. Black PRies   d. Convergent

Chapter 4. Customer Relationship Management and the Marketing Research Process

1. _____ refer to a collection of facts usually collected as the result of experience, observation or experiment or a set of premises. This may consist of numbers, words particularly as measurements or observations of a set of variables. _____ are often viewed as a lowest level of abstraction from which information and knowledge are derived.
   a. Data
   b. Pearson product-moment correlation coefficient
   c. Sample size
   d. Mean

2. _____ is the process of extracting hidden patterns from data. As more data is gathered, with the amount of data doubling every three years, _____ is becoming an increasingly important tool to transform this data into information. It is commonly used in a wide range of profiling practices, such as marketing, surveillance, fraud detection and scientific discovery.
   a. Power III
   b. Structure mining
   c. 180SearchAssistant
   d. Data mining

3. A _____ is a structured collection of records or data that is stored in a computer system. The structure is achieved by organizing the data according to a _____ model. The model in most common use today is the relational model.
   a. Power III
   b. 6-3-5 Brainwriting
   c. 180SearchAssistant
   d. Database

4. In marketing, customer _____, lifetime customer value (LCV), or _____ (LTV) and a new concept of 'customer life cycle management' is the present value of the future cash flows attributed to the customer relationship. Use of customer _____ as a marketing metric tends to place greater emphasis on customer service and long-term customer satisfaction, rather than on maximizing short-term sales.

   Customer _____ has intuitive appeal as a marketing concept, because in theory it represents exactly how much each customer is worth in monetary terms, and therefore exactly how much a marketing department should be willing to spend to acquire each customer.

   a. Sweepstakes
   b. Value chain
   c. Brand infiltration
   d. Lifetime value

5. A personal and cultural _____ is a relative ethic _____, an assumption upon which implementation can be extrapolated. A _____ system is a set of consistent _____s and measures that is soo not true. A principle _____ is a foundation upon which other _____s and measures of integrity are based.
   a. Package-on-Package
   b. Perceptual maps
   c. Value
   d. Supreme Court of the United States

6. _____ consists of the processes a company uses to track and organize its contacts with its current and prospective customers. _____ software is used to support these processes; information about customers and customer interactions can be entered, stored and accessed by employees in different company departments. Typical _____ goals are to improve services provided to customers, and to use customer contact information for targeted marketing.
   a. Product bundling
   b. Commercialization
   c. Demand generation
   d. Customer relationship management

7. _____ is a form of marketing developed from direct response marketing campaigns conducted in the 1970's and 1980's which emphasizes customer retention and satisfaction, rather than a dominant focus on 'point of sale' transactions.

Chapter 4. Customer Relationship Management and the Marketing Research Process

_____ differs from other forms of marketing in that it recognizes the long term value to the firm of keeping customers, as opposed to direct or 'Intrusion' marketing, which focuses upon acquisition of new clients by targeting majority demographics based upon prospective client lists.

_____ refers to long-term and mutually beneficial arrangement wherein both buyer and seller focus on value enhancement through the certain of more satisfying exchange. This approach attempts to transcend the simple purchase exchange process with customer to make more meaningful and richer contact by providing a more holistic, personalized purchase, and use orn consumption experience to create stronger ties.

a. Relationship marketing
b. Diversity marketing
c. Global marketing
d. Guerrilla Marketing

8. _____ is defined by the American _____ Association as the activity, set of institutions, and processes for creating, communicating, delivering, and exchanging offerings that have value for customers, clients, partners, and society at large. The term developed from the original meaning which referred literally to going to market, as in shopping, or going to a market to sell goods or services.

_____ practice tends to be seen as a creative industry, which includes advertising, distribution and selling.

a. Customer acquisition management
b. Product naming
c. Marketing
d. Marketing myopia

9. Customer _____ consists of the processes a company uses to track and organize its contacts with its current and prospective customers. CRelationship management software is used to support these processes; information about customers and customer interactions can be entered, stored and accessed by employees in different company departments. Typical CRelationship management goals are to improve services provided to customers, and to use customer contact information for targeted marketing.

a. Green marketing
b. Relationship management
c. Product bundling
d. Marketing

10. _____, a business term, is a measure of how products and services supplied by a company meet or surpass customer expectation. It is seen as a key performance indicator within business and is part of the four perspectives of a Balanced Scorecard.

In a competitive marketplace where businesses compete for customers, _____ is seen as a key differentiator and increasingly has become a key element of business strategy.

a. Customer satisfaction
b. Psychological pricing
c. Supplier diversity
d. Customer base

11. _____ is the activity that the selling organization undertakes to reduce customer account defections. The success of this activity is when the customer account places an additional order before a 12-month period has expired. Note that ideally these orders will need to contribute similar financial amounts to the previous 12 months.

Chapter 4. Customer Relationship Management and the Marketing Research Process

a. First-mover advantage
c. Customer centricity
b. Customer base
d. Customer retention

12. _____ is a process of gathering, modeling, and transforming data with the goal of highlighting useful information, suggesting conclusions, and supporting decision making. _____ has multiple facets and approaches, encompassing diverse techniques under a variety of names, in different business, science, and social science domains.

Data mining is a particular _____ technique that focuses on modeling and knowledge discovery for predictive rather than purely descriptive purposes.

a. Data analysis
c. Power III
b. 180SearchAssistant
d. 6-3-5 Brainwriting

13. Competitiveness is a comparative concept of the ability and performance of a firm, sub-sector or country to sell and supply goods and/or services in a given market. Although widely used in economics and business management, the usefulness of the concept, particularly in the context of national competitiveness, is vigorously disputed by economists, such as Paul Krugman .

The term may also be applied to markets, where it is used to refer to the extent to which the market structure may be regarded as perfectly _____.

a. Customs union
c. Competitive
b. Geographical pricing
d. Free trade zone

14. In statistics, an _____ is a term in a statistical model added when the effect of two or more variables is not simply additive. Such a term reflects that the effect of one variable depends on the values of one or more other variables.

Thus, for a response Y and two variables x_1 and x_2 an additive model would be:

$$Y = ax_1 + bx_2 + \text{error}$$

In contrast to this,

$$Y = ax_1 + bx_2 + c(x_1 \times x_2) + \text{error},$$

is an example of a model with an _____ between variables x_1 and x_2 ('error' refers to the random variable whose value by which y differs from the expected value of y.)

a. Interaction
c. ADTECH
b. AMAX
d. ACNielsen

Chapter 4. Customer Relationship Management and the Marketing Research Process

15. _____s are used in open sentences. For instance, in the formula x + 1 = 5, x is a _____ which represents an 'unknown' number. _____s are often represented by letters of the Roman alphabet, or those of other alphabets, such as Greek, and use other special symbols.

   a. Book of business
   b. Personalization
   c. Quantitative
   d. Variable

16. _____ is an American firm that measures media audiences, including television, radio, theatre films (via the AMC MAP program) and newspapers. _____, headquartered in New York City and operating primarily from Chicago, is best-known for the Nielsen Ratings, a measurement of television viewership.

   _____, the preeminent media research company in the world, began as a division of ACNielsen, a marketing research firm.

   a. CoolBrands
   b. Nielsen Media Research
   c. Hennes ' Mauritz
   d. Green Earth Market

17. _____ is a term used to describe a process of preparing and collecting data - for example as part of a process improvement or similar project.

   _____ usually takes place early on in an improvement project, and is often formalised through a _____ Plan which often contains the following activity.

   1. Pre collection activity - Agree goals, target data, definitions, methods
   2. Collection - _____
   3. Present Findings - usually involves some form of sorting analysis and/or presentation.

   A formal _____ process is necessary as it ensures that data gathered is both defined and accurate and that subsequent decisions based on arguments embodied in the findings are valid . The process provides both a baseline from which to measure from and in certain cases a target on what to improve. Types of _____ 1-By mail questionnaires 2-By personal interview

   - Six sigma
   - Sampling (statistics)

   a. 6-3-5 Brainwriting
   b. 180SearchAssistant
   c. Power III
   d. Data collection

18. Combining Existing _____ Sources with New Primary Data Sources

Imagine that we could get hold of a good collection of surveys taken in earlier years, such as detailed studies about changes going on in this phase and hopefully additional studies in the years to come. Analyzing this data base over time could give us a good picture of what changes actually have taken place in the orientation of the population and of the extent to which new technical concepts did have an impact on subgroups of the population. Furthermore, data archives can help to prepare studies on change over time by monitoring what questions have been asked in earlier years and alerting principal investigators to important questions which should be repeated in planned research projects.

a. Power III
b. 6-3-5 Brainwriting
c. 180SearchAssistant
d. Secondary data

19. _____ , according to Cornish, 'the process of acquiring and analyzing information in order to understand the market (both existing and potential customers); to determine the current and future needs and preferences, attitudes and behavior of the market; and to assess changes in the business environment that may affect the size and nature of the market in the future.' ('Product', 1997, p147.)

This figure shows how the interaction between variables from producers, communication channels, and consumers vary the effectiveness of _____ which affects the performance of the sales of a new product. The product is central in a circle because it helps to direct what information is gathered and how.

a. Market intelligence
b. Brand parity
c. Co-branding
d. Line extension

20. Consumer market research is a form of applied sociology that concentrates on understanding the behaviours, whims and preferences, of consumers in a market-based economy, and aims to understand the effects and comparative success of marketing campaigns. The field of consumer _____ as a statistical science was pioneered by Arthur Nielsen with the founding of the ACNielsen Company in 1923 .

Thus _____ is the systematic and objective identification, collection, analysis, and dissemination of information for the purpose of assisting management in decision making related to the identification and solution of problems and opportunities in marketing.

a. Focus group
b. Marketing research process
c. Logit analysis
d. Marketing Research

21. A _____ is a research instrument consisting of a series of questions and other prompts for the purpose of gathering information from respondents. Although they are often designed for statistical analysis of the responses, this is not always the case. The _____ was invented by Sir Francis Galton.
a. Mystery shopping
b. Market research
c. Mystery shoppers
d. Questionnaire

22. _____ is the use of an object (typically referred to as an RFID tag) applied to or incorporated into a product, animal, or person for the purpose of identification and tracking using radio waves. Some tags can be read from several meters away and beyond the line of sight of the reader.

Chapter 4. Customer Relationship Management and the Marketing Research Process 47

Most RFID tags contain at least two parts.

    a. 180SearchAssistant
    b. Power III
    c. 6-3-5 Brainwriting
    d. Radio-frequency identification

23. _____ is that part of statistical practice concerned with the selection of individual observations intended to yield some knowledge about a population of concern, especially for the purposes of statistical inference. Each observation measures one or more properties (weight, location, etc.) of an observable entity enumerated to distinguish objects or individuals.
    a. Richard Buckminster 'Bucky' Fuller
    b. Sports Marketing Group
    c. AStore
    d. Sampling

24. _____ a research method involving the use of questionnaires and/or statistical surveys to gather data about people and their thoughts and behaviours.
    a. Z-test
    b. Survey research
    c. T-test
    d. Control chart

25. Human beings are also considered to be _____ because they have the ability to change raw materials into valuable _____. The term Human _____ can also be defined as the skills, energies, talents, abilities and knowledge that are used for the production of goods or the rendering of services. While taking into account human beings as _____, the following things have to be kept in mind:

- The size of the population
- The capabilities of the individuals in that population

Many _____ cannot be consumed in their original form. They have to be processed in order to change them into more usable commodities.

    a. 6-3-5 Brainwriting
    b. Power III
    c. 180SearchAssistant
    d. Resources

26. A _____ is a documented investigation of a Market that is used to inform a firm's planning activities particularly around decision of: inventory, purchase, work force expansion/contraction, facility expansion, purchases of capital equipment, promotional activities, and many other aspects of a company.

Not all managers are asked to conduct a _____, but all managers must make decisions using _____ data and understand how the data was derived. So all managers need a reasonable understanding of the tools most used for making sales forecasts and analyzing markets.

    a. Simple random sampling
    b. Market analysis
    c. Cross tabulation
    d. Preference regression

Chapter 4. Customer Relationship Management and the Marketing Research Process

27. A _____ is a subgroup of people or organizations sharing one or more characteristics that cause them to have similar product and/or service needs. A true _____ meets all of the following criteria: it is distinct from other segments (different segments have different needs), it is homogeneous within the segment (exhibits common needs); it responds similarly to a market stimulus, and it can be reached by a market intervention. The term is also used when consumers with identical product and/or service needs are divided up into groups so they can be charged different amounts.
   a. Customer insight
   b. Commercial planning
   c. Production orientation
   d. Market segment

28. Procter is a surname, and may also refer to:

   - Bryan Waller Procter (pseud. Barry Cornwall), English poet
   - Goodwin Procter, American law firm
   - _____, consumer products multinational

   a. Procter ' Gamble
   b. Convergent
   c. Black PRies
   d. Flyer

29. _____ is a term for unprocessed data, it is also known as primary data. It is a relative term _____ can be input to a computer program or used in manual analysis procedures such as gathering statistics from a survey.
   a. Shoppers Food ' Pharmacy
   b. Product manager
   c. Chief marketing officer
   d. Raw data

30. _____ is a method used for analyzing customer behavior and defining market segments. It is commonly used in database marketing and direct marketing and has received particular attention in retail.

   _____ stands for

   - Recency - When was the last order?
   - Frequency - How many orders have they placed with us?
   - Monetary Value - What is the value of their orders?

   To create an _____ analysis, one creates categories for each attribute. For instance, the Recency attribute might be broken into three categories: customers with purchases within the last 90 days; between 91 and 365 days; and longer than 365 days.

   a. RFM
   b. Retail loss prevention
   c. Merchant
   d. Trade credit

31. A _____ is a commercial building for storage of goods. _____s are used by manufacturers, importers, exporters, wholesalers, transport businesses, customs, etc. They are usually large plain buildings in industrial areas of cities and towns.
   a. 180SearchAssistant
   b. 6-3-5 Brainwriting
   c. Power III
   d. Warehouse

Chapter 4. Customer Relationship Management and the Marketing Research Process

32. The loyalty business model is a business model used in strategic management in which company resources are employed so as to increase the loyalty of customers and other stakeholders in the expectation that corporate objectives will be met or surpassed. A typical example of this type of model is: quality of product or service leads to customer satisfaction, which leads to _____, which leads to profitability.

Fredrick Reichheld (1996) expanded the loyalty business model beyond customers and employees.

    a. 6-3-5 Brainwriting   b. Power III
    c. Customer loyalty   d. 180SearchAssistant

33. In marketing generally and in retailing more specifically, a _____, rewards card, points card, advantage card visually similar to a credit card or debit card, that identifies the card holder as a member in a loyalty program. _____s are a system of the loyalty business model. In the United Kingdom it is typically called a _____, in Canada a rewards card or a points card, and in the United States either a discount card, a club card or a rewards card.

    a. Power III   b. 180SearchAssistant
    c. 6-3-5 Brainwriting   d. Loyalty card

34. A _____ is a statement or claim that a particular event will occur in the future in more certain terms than a forecast. The etymology of this word is Latin . In regards to predicting the future Howard H. Stevenson Says, ' _____ is at least two things: Important and hard.' Important, because we have to act, and hard because we have to realize the future we want, and what is the best way to get there.

    a. 6-3-5 Brainwriting   b. 180SearchAssistant
    c. Power III   d. Prediction

35. _____ is the realization of an application idea, model, design, specification, standard, algorithm an _____ is a realization of a technical specification or algorithm as a program, software component, or other computer system. Many _____s may exist for a given specification or standard.

    a. ACNielsen   b. AMAX
    c. ADTECH   d. Implementation

Chapter 4. Customer Relationship Management and the Marketing Research Process

36. A number of different _____s are indicated below.

- Randomized controlled trial
    - Double-blind randomized trial
    - Single-blind randomized trial
    - Non-blind trial
- Nonrandomized trial (quasi-experiment)
    - Interrupted time series design (measures on a sample or a series of samples from the same population are obtained several times before and after a manipulated event or a naturally occurring event) - considered a type of quasi-experiment

- Cohort study
    - Prospective cohort
    - Retrospective cohort
    - Time series study
- Case-control study
    - Nested case-control study
- Cross-sectional study
    - Community survey (a type of cross-sectional study)

When choosing a _____, many factors must be taken into account. Different types of studies are subject to different types of bias. For example, recall bias is likely to occur in cross-sectional or case-control studies where subjects are asked to recall exposure to risk factors.

a. 180SearchAssistant
b. Longitudinal studies
c. Power III
d. Study design

37. _____ is a form of communication that typically attempts to persuade potential customers to purchase or to consume more of a particular brand of product or service. 'While now central to the contemporary global economy and the reproduction of global production networks, it is only quite recently that _____ has been more than a marginal influence on patterns of sales and production. The formation of modern _____ was intimately bound up with the emergence of new forms of monopoly capitalism around the end of the 19th and beginning of the 20th century as one element in corporate strategies to create, organize and where possible control markets, especially for mass produced consumer goods.

a. ADTECH
b. ACNielsen
c. AMAX
d. Advertising

38. The _____ is an American federal law (codified at 15 U.S.C. § 1681 et seq.) that regulates the collection, dissemination, and use of consumer credit information.

a. Power III
b. 180SearchAssistant
c. Fair Credit Reporting Act
d. 6-3-5 Brainwriting

39. _____ is either an activity of a living being (such as a human), consisting of receiving knowledge of the outside world through the senses, or the recording of data using scientific instruments. The term may also refer to any datum collected during this activity.

The scientific method requires _____s of nature to formulate and test hypotheses.

a. ADTECH
c. AMAX
b. ACNielsen
d. Observation

Chapter 5. Marketing Decision Support Systems

1. _____ consists of the processes a company uses to track and organize its contacts with its current and prospective customers. _____ software is used to support these processes; information about customers and customer interactions can be entered, stored and accessed by employees in different company departments. Typical _____ goals are to improve services provided to customers, and to use customer contact information for targeted marketing.
   a. Customer relationship management
   b. Commercialization
   c. Demand generation
   d. Product bundling

2. _____ is defined by the American _____ Association as the activity, set of institutions, and processes for creating, communicating, delivering, and exchanging offerings that have value for customers, clients, partners, and society at large. The term developed from the original meaning which referred literally to going to market, as in shopping, or going to a market to sell goods or services.

   _____ practice tends to be seen as a creative industry, which includes advertising, distribution and selling.

   a. Marketing myopia
   b. Marketing
   c. Product naming
   d. Customer acquisition management

3. _____ is a form of marketing developed from direct response marketing campaigns conducted in the 1970's and 1980's which emphasizes customer retention and satisfaction, rather than a dominant focus on 'point of sale' transactions.

   _____ differs from other forms of marketing in that it recognizes the long term value to the firm of keeping customers, as opposed to direct or 'Intrusion' marketing, which focuses upon acquisition of new clients by targeting majority demographics based upon prospective client lists.

   _____ refers to long-term and mutually beneficial arrangement wherein both buyer and seller focus on value enhancement through the certain of more satisfying exchange. This approach attempts to transcend the simple purchase exchange process with customer to make more meaningful and richer contact by providing a more holistic, personalized purchase, and use orn consumption experience to create stronger ties.

   a. Diversity marketing
   b. Global marketing
   c. Guerrilla Marketing
   d. Relationship marketing

4. _____ is the activity that the selling organization undertakes to reduce customer account defections. The success of this activity is when the customer account places an additional order before a 12-month period has expired. Note that ideally these orders will need to contribute similar financial amounts to the previous 12 months.
   a. First-mover advantage
   b. Customer retention
   c. Customer centricity
   d. Customer base

5. A _____ is a structured collection of records or data that is stored in a computer system. The structure is achieved by organizing the data according to a _____ model. The model in most common use today is the relational model.
   a. Power III
   b. 180SearchAssistant
   c. Database
   d. 6-3-5 Brainwriting

Chapter 5. Marketing Decision Support Systems

6. Customer _____ consists of the processes a company uses to track and organize its contacts with its current and prospective customers. CRelationship management software is used to support these processes; information about customers and customer interactions can be entered, stored and accessed by employees in different company departments. Typical CRelationship management goals are to improve services provided to customers, and to use customer contact information for targeted marketing.

   a. Product bundling
   b. Green marketing
   c. Relationship management
   d. Marketing

7. A _____, in the field of business and marketing, is a geographic region or demographic group used to gauge the viability of a product or service in the mass market prior to a wide scale roll-out. The criteria used to judge the acceptability of a _____ region or group include:

   1. a population that is demographically similar to the proposed target market; and
   2. relative isolation from densely populated media markets so that advertising to the test audience can be efficient and economical.

The _____ ideally aims to duplicate 'everything' - promotion and distribution as well as `product' - on a smaller scale. The technique replicates, typically in one area, what is planned to occur in a national launch; and the results are very carefully monitored, so that they can be extrapolated to projected national results. The `area' may be any one of the following:

- Television area
- Test town
- Residential neighborhood
- Test site

A number of decisions have to be taken about any _____:

- Which _____?
- What is to be tested?
- How long a test?
- What are the success criteria?

The simple go or no-go decision, together with the related reduction of risk, is normally the main justification for the expense of _____s. At the same time, however, such _____s can be used to test specific elements of a new product's marketing mix; possibly the version of the product itself, the promotional message and media spend, the distribution channels and the price.

   a. Test market
   b. Preadolescence
   c. Power III
   d. 180SearchAssistant

8. _____ refer to a collection of facts usually collected as the result of experience, observation or experiment or a set of premises. This may consist of numbers, words particularly as measurements or observations of a set of variables. _____ are often viewed as a lowest level of abstraction from which information and knowledge are derived.

a. Mean
b. Pearson product-moment correlation coefficient
c. Sample size
d. Data

9. _____ is a type of research conducted because a problem has not been clearly defined. _____ helps determine the best research design, data collection method and selection of subjects. Given its fundamental nature, _____ often concludes that a perceived problem does not actually exist.
   a. ACNielsen
   b. Intent scale translation
   c. IDDEA
   d. Exploratory research

10. A number of different _____s are indicated below.

   - Randomized controlled trial
     - Double-blind randomized trial
     - Single-blind randomized trial
     - Non-blind trial
   - Nonrandomized trial (quasi-experiment)
     - Interrupted time series design (measures on a sample or a series of samples from the same population are obtained several times before and after a manipulated event or a naturally occurring event) - considered a type of quasi-experiment

   - Cohort study
     - Prospective cohort
     - Retrospective cohort
     - Time series study
   - Case-control study
     - Nested case-control study
   - Cross-sectional study
     - Community survey (a type of cross-sectional study)

When choosing a _____, many factors must be taken into account. Different types of studies are subject to different types of bias. For example, recall bias is likely to occur in cross-sectional or case-control studies where subjects are asked to recall exposure to risk factors.

   a. Power III
   b. 180SearchAssistant
   c. Longitudinal studies
   d. Study design

11. A personal and cultural _____ is a relative ethic _____, an assumption upon which implementation can be extrapolated. A _____ system is a set of consistent _____s and measures that is soo not true. A principle _____ is a foundation upon which other _____s and measures of integrity are based.
   a. Package-on-Package
   b. Perceptual maps
   c. Supreme Court of the United States
   d. Value

12. _____ constitute a class of computer-based information systems including knowledge-based systems that support decision-making activities.

Chapter 5. Marketing Decision Support Systems

_____ are a specific class of computerized information system that supports business and organizational decision-making activities. A properly-designed _____ is an interactive software-based system intended to help decision makers compile useful information from raw data, documents, personal knowledge, and/or business models to identify and solve problems and make decisions.

   a. 6-3-5 Brainwriting   b. Power III
   c. 180SearchAssistant   d. Decision Support Systems

13. A _____ is a type of bar chart that illustrates a project schedule. A _____ illustrates the start and finish dates of the terminal elements and summary elements of a project. Terminal elements and summary elements comprise the work breakdown structure of the project.

   a. 180SearchAssistant   b. Power III
   c. Gantt chart   d. 6-3-5 Brainwriting

14. _____ is an information system that helps with decision-making in the formation of a marketing plan. The reason for using an MKDSS is because it helps to support the software vendors' planning strategy for marketing products; it can help to identify advantageous levels of pricing, advertising spending, and advertising copy for the firm's products (Arinze, 1990.) This helps determines the firms marketing mix for product software.

   a. Marketing Decision Support Systems   b. 6-3-5 Brainwriting
   c. Power III   d. 180SearchAssistant

15. _____ is the imitation of some real thing, state of affairs, or process. The act of simulating something generally entails representing certain key characteristics or behaviors of a selected physical or abstract system.

_____ is used in many contexts, including the modeling of natural systems or human systems in order to gain insight into their functioning.

   a. Simulation   b. Power III
   c. 180SearchAssistant   d. 6-3-5 Brainwriting

16. _____ is the study of the Earth and its lands, features, inhabitants, and phenomena. A literal translation would be 'to describe or write about the Earth'. The first person to use the word '_____' was Eratosthenes .

   a. 180SearchAssistant   b. 6-3-5 Brainwriting
   c. Power III   d. Geography

17. A _____ captures, stores, analyzes, manages, and presents data that is linked to location.

In the strictest sense, the term describes any information system that integrates, stores, edits, analyzes, shares, and displays geographic information. In a more generic sense, _____ applications are tools that allow users to create interactive queries (user created searches), analyze spatial information, edit data, maps, and present the results of all these operations.

   a. Geographic information system   b. Power III
   c. 6-3-5 Brainwriting   d. 180SearchAssistant

Chapter 5. Marketing Decision Support Systems

18. A supply chain is the system of organizations, people, technology, activities, information and resources involved in moving a product or service from _____ to customer. Supply chain activities transform natural resources, raw materials and components into a finished product that is delivered to the end customer. In sophisticated supply chain systems, used products may re-enter the supply chain at any point where residual value is recyclable.

   a. Bringin' Home the Oil
   b. Rebate
   c. Product line extension
   d. Supplier

19. _____ is one of the four elements of marketing mix. An organization or set of organizations (go-betweens) involved in the process of making a product or service available for use or consumption by a consumer or business user.

The other three parts of the marketing mix are product, pricing, and promotion.

   a. Better Living Through Chemistry
   b. Comparison-Shopping agent
   c. Japan Advertising Photographers' Association
   d. Distribution

20. Consumer market research is a form of applied sociology that concentrates on understanding the behaviours, whims and preferences, of consumers in a market-based economy, and aims to understand the effects and comparative success of marketing campaigns. The field of consumer _____ as a statistical science was pioneered by Arthur Nielsen with the founding of the ACNielsen Company in 1923.

Thus _____ is the systematic and objective identification, collection, analysis, and dissemination of information for the purpose of assisting management in decision making related to the identification and solution of problems and opportunities in marketing.

   a. Logit analysis
   b. Marketing research process
   c. Marketing research
   d. Focus group

21. _____ is a set of six steps which defines the tasks to be accomplished in conducting a marketing research study. These include problem definition, developing an approach to problem, research design formulation, field work, data preparation and analysis, and report generation and presentation.

   a. Preference-rank translation
   b. Market analysis
   c. Marketing research process
   d. Simple random sampling

22. Combining Existing _____ Sources with New Primary Data Sources

Imagine that we could get hold of a good collection of surveys taken in earlier years, such as detailed studies about changes going on in this phase and hopefully additional studies in the years to come. Analyzing this data base over time could give us a good picture of what changes actually have taken place in the orientation of the population and of the extent to which new technical concepts did have an impact on subgroups of the population. Furthermore, data archives can help to prepare studies on change over time by monitoring what questions have been asked in earlier years and alerting principal investigators to important questions which should be repeated in planned research projects.

   a. Power III
   b. 6-3-5 Brainwriting
   c. Secondary data
   d. 180SearchAssistant

Chapter 5. Marketing Decision Support Systems

23. _____ is systematic determination of merit, worth, and significance of something or someone using criteria against a set of standards. _____ often is used to characterize and appraise subjects of interest in a wide range of human enterprises, including the arts, criminal justice, foundations and non-profit organizations, government, health care, and other human services.

Depending on the topic of interest, there are professional groups which look to the quality and rigor of the _____ process.

    a. ACNielsen   b. ADTECH
    c. AMAX   d. Evaluation

24. A _____ is a retail establishment which specializes in selling a wide range of products without a single predominant merchandise line. _____s usually sell products including apparel, furniture, appliances, electronics, and additionally select other lines of products such as paint, hardware, toiletries, cosmetics, photographic equipment, jewelery, toys, and sporting goods. Certain _____s are further classified as discount _____s.

    a. Power III   b. 6-3-5 Brainwriting
    c. 180SearchAssistant   d. Department Store

25. _____ is a form of communication that typically attempts to persuade potential customers to purchase or to consume more of a particular brand of product or service. 'While now central to the contemporary global economy and the reproduction of global production networks, it is only quite recently that _____ has been more than a marginal influence on patterns of sales and production. The formation of modern _____ was intimately bound up with the emergence of new forms of monopoly capitalism around the end of the 19th and beginning of the 20th century as one element in corporate strategies to create, organize and where possible control markets, especially for mass produced consumer goods.

    a. ACNielsen   b. AMAX
    c. ADTECH   d. Advertising

26. _____ refers to the structured transmission of data between organizations by electronic means. It is used to transfer electronic documents from one computer system to another (ie) from one trading partner to another trading partner. It is more than mere E-mail; for instance, organizations might replace bills of lading and even checks with appropriate _____ messages.

    a. AMAX   b. ADTECH
    c. ACNielsen   d. Electronic data interchange

27. _____ is an advertisement in which a particular product specifically mentions a competitor by name for the express purpose of showing why the competitor is inferior to the product naming it.

This should not be confused with parody advertisements, where a fictional product is being advertised for the purpose of poking fun at the particular advertisement, nor should it be confused with the use of a coined brand name for the purpose of comparing the product without actually naming an actual competitor. ('Wikipedia tastes better and is less filling than the Encyclopedia Galactica.')

In the 1980s, during what has been referred to as the cola wars, soft-drink manufacturer Pepsi ran a series of advertisements where people, caught on hidden camera, in a blind taste test, chose Pepsi over rival Coca-Cola.

Chapter 5. Marketing Decision Support Systems

a. Cost per conversion
b. GL-70
c. Heavy-up
d. Comparative advertising

28. _____ is either an activity of a living being (such as a human), consisting of receiving knowledge of the outside world through the senses, or the recording of data using scientific instruments. The term may also refer to any datum collected during this activity.

The scientific method requires _____s of nature to formulate and test hypotheses.

a. ADTECH
b. Observation
c. ACNielsen
d. AMAX

29. Procter is a surname, and may also refer to:

- Bryan Waller Procter (pseud. Barry Cornwall), English poet
- Goodwin Procter, American law firm
- _____, consumer products multinational

a. Convergent
b. Flyer
c. Black PRies
d. Procter ' Gamble

30. _____ generally refers to a list of all planned expenses and revenues. It is a plan for saving and spending. A _____ is an important concept in microeconomics, which uses a _____ line to illustrate the trade-offs between two or more goods.

a. Power III
b. Budget
c. 6-3-5 Brainwriting
d. 180SearchAssistant

31. _____ is the process of estimation in unknown situations. Prediction is a similar, but more general term. Both can refer to estimation of time series, cross-sectional or longitudinal data.

a. 6-3-5 Brainwriting
b. 180SearchAssistant
c. Forecasting
d. Power III

32. _____ is a term used by project managers and project management (PM) organizations to describe methods for analyzing and collectively managing a group of current or proposed projects based on numerous key characteristics. The fundamental objective of the _____ process is to determine the optimal mix and sequencing of proposed projects to best achieve the organization's overall goals - typically expressed in terms of hard economic measures, business strategy goals, or technical strategy goals - while honoring constraints imposed by management or external real-world factors. Typical attributes of projects being analyzed in a _____ process include each project's total expected cost, consumption of scarce resources (human or otherwise) expected timeline and schedule of investment, expected nature, magnitude and timing of benefits to be realized, and relationship or inter-dependencies with other projects in the portfolio.

a. Power III
b. Pop-up ads
c. Project Portfolio Management
d. Customer intelligence

33. _____ is a computer program used for statistical analysis.

Chapter 5. Marketing Decision Support Systems

_____ (originally, Statistical Package for the Social Sciences) was released in its first version in 1968 after being founded by Norman Nie and C. Hadlai Hull. Nie was then a political science postgraduate at Stanford University, and now Research Professor in the Department of Political Science at Stanford and Professor Emeritus of Political Science at the University of Chicago.

a. 6-3-5 Brainwriting
b. Power III
c. SPSS
d. 180SearchAssistant

34. The _____ is a global navigation satellite system (GNSS) developed by the United States Department of Defense and managed by the United States Air Force 50th Space Wing. It is the only fully functional GNSS in the world, can be used freely, and is often used by civilians for navigation purposes. It uses a constellation of between 24 and 32 Medium Earth Orbit satellites that transmit precise microwave signals, which allow _____ receivers to determine their current location, the time, and their velocity.

a. 6-3-5 Brainwriting
b. Power III
c. 180SearchAssistant
d. Global Positioning System

35. In marketing, _____ has come to mean the process by which marketers try to create an image or identity in the minds of their target market for its product, brand, or organization. It is the 'relative competitive comparison' their product occupies in a given market as perceived by the target market.

Re-_____ involves changing the identity of a product, relative to the identity of competing products, in the collective minds of the target market.

a. Positioning
b. GE matrix
c. Moratorium
d. Containerization

36. _____ is a rivalry between individuals, groups, nations for territory, a niche, or allocation of resources. It arises whenever two or more parties strive for a goal which cannot be shared. _____ occurs naturally between living organisms which co-exist in the same environment.

a. Non-price competition
b. Price competition
c. Price fixing
d. Competition

37. The general definition of an _____ is an evaluation of a person, organization, system, process, project or product. _____s are performed to ascertain the validity and reliability of information; also to provide an assessment of a system's internal control. The goal of an _____ is to express an opinion on the person/organization/system (etc) in question, under evaluation based on work done on a test basis.

a. AMAX
b. ACNielsen
c. Audit
d. ADTECH

38. Competitiveness is a comparative concept of the ability and performance of a firm, sub-sector or country to sell and supply goods and/or services in a given market. Although widely used in economics and business management, the usefulness of the concept, particularly in the context of national competitiveness, is vigorously disputed by economists, such as Paul Krugman .

The term may also be applied to markets, where it is used to refer to the extent to which the market structure may be regarded as perfectly _____.

a. Competitive
b. Free trade zone
c. Customs union
d. Geographical pricing

39. Human beings are also considered to be _____ because they have the ability to change raw materials into valuable _____. The term Human _____ can also be defined as the skills, energies, talents, abilities and knowledge that are used for the production of goods or the rendering of services. While taking into account human beings as _____, the following things have to be kept in mind:

- The size of the population
- The capabilities of the individuals in that population

Many _____ cannot be consumed in their original form. They have to be processed in order to change them into more usable commodities.

a. 180SearchAssistant
b. 6-3-5 Brainwriting
c. Power III
d. Resources

40. _____ is the process of comparing the cost, cycle time, productivity, or quality of a specific process or method to another that is widely considered to be an industry standard or best practice. The result is often a business case for making changes in order to make improvements. The term _____ was first used by cobblers to measure ones feet for shoes.

a. Switching cost
b. Benchmarking
c. Business strategy
d. Strategic group

41. _____ is the process of extracting hidden patterns from data. As more data is gathered, with the amount of data doubling every three years, _____ is becoming an increasingly important tool to transform this data into information. It is commonly used in a wide range of profiling practices, such as marketing, surveillance, fraud detection and scientific discovery.

a. 180SearchAssistant
b. Data mining
c. Structure mining
d. Power III

42. In marketing, customer _____, lifetime customer value (LCV), or _____ (LTV) and a new concept of 'customer life cycle management' is the present value of the future cash flows attributed to the customer relationship. Use of customer _____ as a marketing metric tends to place greater emphasis on customer service and long-term customer satisfaction, rather than on maximizing short-term sales.

Customer _____ has intuitive appeal as a marketing concept, because in theory it represents exactly how much each customer is worth in monetary terms, and therefore exactly how much a marketing department should be willing to spend to acquire each customer.

a. Lifetime value
b. Sweepstakes
c. Value chain
d. Brand infiltration

43. A _____ is a process that can allow an organization to concentrate its limited resources on the greatest opportunities to increase sales and achieve a sustainable competitive advantage. A _____ should be centered around the key concept that customer satisfaction is the main goal.

A _____ is most effective when it is an integral component of corporate strategy, defining how the organization will successfully engage customers, prospects, and competitors in the market arena.

   a. Cyberdoc
   c. Psychographic
   b. Societal marketing
   d. Marketing strategy

44. A _____ is a plan of action designed to achieve a particular goal.

_____ is different from tactics. In military terms, tactics is concerned with the conduct of an engagement while _____ is concerned with how different engagements are linked.

   a. 6-3-5 Brainwriting
   c. Strategy
   b. Power III
   d. 180SearchAssistant

45. In probability theory and statistics, _____ indicates the strength and direction of a linear relationship between two random variables. That is in contrast with the usage of the term in colloquial speech, denoting any relationship, not necessarily linear. In general statistical usage, _____ or co-relation refers to the departure of two random variables from independence.
   a. Correlation
   c. Frequency distribution
   b. Mean
   d. Probability

Chapter 6. Exploratory Designs: In-Depth Interviews and Focus Groups

1. _____ is a type of research conducted because a problem has not been clearly defined. _____ helps determine the best research design, data collection method and selection of subjects. Given its fundamental nature, _____ often concludes that a perceived problem does not actually exist.
   a. IDDEA
   b. ACNielsen
   c. Intent scale translation
   d. Exploratory research

2. _____ is a field of inquiry that crosscuts disciplines and subject matters. _____ers aim to gather an in-depth understanding of human behavior and the reasons that govern such behavior. The discipline investigates the why and how of decision making, not just what, where, when.
   a. 180SearchAssistant
   b. Qualitative research
   c. Power III
   d. 6-3-5 Brainwriting

3. A number of different _____s are indicated below.

   - Randomized controlled trial
     - Double-blind randomized trial
     - Single-blind randomized trial
     - Non-blind trial
   - Nonrandomized trial (quasi-experiment)
     - Interrupted time series design (measures on a sample or a series of samples from the same population are obtained several times before and after a manipulated event or a naturally occurring event) - considered a type of quasi-experiment

   - Cohort study
     - Prospective cohort
     - Retrospective cohort
     - Time series study
   - Case-control study
     - Nested case-control study
   - Cross-sectional study
     - Community survey (a type of cross-sectional study)

   When choosing a _____, many factors must be taken into account. Different types of studies are subject to different types of bias. For example, recall bias is likely to occur in cross-sectional or case-control studies where subjects are asked to recall exposure to risk factors.

   a. 180SearchAssistant
   b. Study design
   c. Power III
   d. Longitudinal studies

4. A _____ is a structured collection of records or data that is stored in a computer system. The structure is achieved by organizing the data according to a _____ model. The model in most common use today is the relational model.
   a. Power III
   b. 6-3-5 Brainwriting
   c. 180SearchAssistant
   d. Database

5. _____ describes data and characteristics about the population or phenomenon being studied. _____ answers the questions who, what, where, when and how.

Chapter 6. Exploratory Designs: In-Depth Interviews and Focus Groups 63

Although the data description is factual, accurate and systematic, the research cannot describe what caused a situation.

a. Power III
b. Two-tailed test
c. Sampling error
d. Descriptive research

6. _____ is a term for unprocessed data, it is also known as primary data. It is a relative term _____ can be input to a computer program or used in manual analysis procedures such as gathering statistics from a survey.

a. Chief marketing officer
b. Product manager
c. Shoppers Food ' Pharmacy
d. Raw data

7. _____ a research method involving the use of questionnaires and/or statistical surveys to gather data about people and their thoughts and behaviours.

a. Control chart
b. Survey research
c. Z-test
d. T-test

8. A _____, in the field of business and marketing, is a geographic region or demographic group used to gauge the viability of a product or service in the mass market prior to a wide scale roll-out. The criteria used to judge the acceptability of a _____ region or group include:

1. a population that is demographically similar to the proposed target market; and
2. relative isolation from densely populated media markets so that advertising to the test audience can be efficient and economical.

The _____ ideally aims to duplicate 'everything' - promotion and distribution as well as `product' - on a smaller scale. The technique replicates, typically in one area, what is planned to occur in a national launch; and the results are very carefully monitored, so that they can be extrapolated to projected national results. The `area' may be any one of the following:

- Television area
- Test town
- Residential neighborhood
- Test site

A number of decisions have to be taken about any _____:

- Which _____?
- What is to be tested?
- How long a test?
- What are the success criteria?

The simple go or no-go decision, together with the related reduction of risk, is normally the main justification for the expense of _____s. At the same time, however, such _____s can be used to test specific elements of a new product's marketing mix; possibly the version of the product itself, the promotional message and media spend, the distribution channels and the price.

    a. Power III
    c. 180SearchAssistant
    b. Preadolescence
    d. Test market

9. _____ is the provision of service to customers before, during and after a purchase.

According to Turban et al., '_____ is a series of activities designed to enhance the level of customer satisfaction - that is, the feeling that a product or service has met the customer expectation.'

Its importance varies by product, industry and customer

    a. Customer experience
    c. Facing
    b. COPC Inc.
    d. Customer service

10. _____ refer to a collection of facts usually collected as the result of experience, observation or experiment or a set of premises. This may consist of numbers, words particularly as measurements or observations of a set of variables. _____ are often viewed as a lowest level of abstraction from which information and knowledge are derived.

    a. Mean
    c. Pearson product-moment correlation coefficient
    b. Sample size
    d. Data

11. _____ is defined by the American _____ Association as the activity, set of institutions, and processes for creating, communicating, delivering, and exchanging offerings that have value for customers, clients, partners, and society at large. The term developed from the original meaning which referred literally to going to market, as in shopping, or going to a market to sell goods or services.

_____ practice tends to be seen as a creative industry, which includes advertising, distribution and selling.

    a. Marketing myopia
    c. Customer acquisition management
    b. Product naming
    d. Marketing

12. _____ is an advertisement in which a particular product specifically mentions a competitor by name for the express purpose of showing why the competitor is inferior to the product naming it.

This should not be confused with parody advertisements, where a fictional product is being advertised for the purpose of poking fun at the particular advertisement, nor should it be confused with the use of a coined brand name for the purpose of comparing the product without actually naming an actual competitor. ('Wikipedia tastes better and is less filling than the Encyclopedia Galactica.')

In the 1980s, during what has been referred to as the cola wars, soft-drink manufacturer Pepsi ran a series of advertisements where people, caught on hidden camera, in a blind taste test, chose Pepsi over rival Coca-Cola.

Chapter 6. Exploratory Designs: In-Depth Interviews and Focus Groups

a. Cost per conversion
b. Comparative advertising
c. Heavy-up
d. GL-70

13. A personal and cultural _____ is a relative ethic _____, an assumption upon which implementation can be extrapolated. A _____ system is a set of consistent _____s and measures that is soo not true. A principle _____ is a foundation upon which other _____s and measures of integrity are based.
    a. Supreme Court of the United States
    b. Package-on-Package
    c. Perceptual maps
    d. Value

14. A _____ attribute is one that exists in a range of magnitudes, and can therefore be measured. Measurements of any particular _____ property are expressed as a specific quantity, referred to as a unit, multiplied by a number. Examples of physical quantities are distance, mass, and time.
    a. Lifestyle city
    b. BeyondROI
    c. Dolly Dimples
    d. Quantitative

15. _____ is a term used to describe a process of preparing and collecting data - for example as part of a process improvement or similar project.

_____ usually takes place early on in an improvement project, and is often formalised through a _____ Plan which often contains the following activity.

1. Pre collection activity - Agree goals, target data, definitions, methods
2. Collection - _____
3. Present Findings - usually involves some form of sorting analysis and/or presentation.

A formal _____ process is necessary as it ensures that data gathered is both defined and accurate and that subsequent decisions based on arguments embodied in the findings are valid . The process provides both a baseline from which to measure from and in certain cases a target on what to improve. Types of _____ 1-By mail questionnaires 2-By personal interview

- Six sigma
- Sampling (statistics)

a. 6-3-5 Brainwriting
b. Power III
c. Data collection
d. 180SearchAssistant

16. _____ is either an activity of a living being (such as a human), consisting of receiving knowledge of the outside world through the senses, or the recording of data using scientific instruments. The term may also refer to any datum collected during this activity.

The scientific method requires _____s of nature to formulate and test hypotheses.

Chapter 6. Exploratory Designs: In-Depth Interviews and Focus Groups

a. AMAX
c. ACNielsen

b. ADTECH
d. Observation

17. _____, a business term, is a measure of how products and services supplied by a company meet or surpass customer expectation. It is seen as a key performance indicator within business and is part of the four perspectives of a Balanced Scorecard.

In a competitive marketplace where businesses compete for customers, _____ is seen as a key differentiator and increasingly has become a key element of business strategy.

a. Psychological pricing
c. Supplier diversity

b. Customer satisfaction
d. Customer base

18. _____ is a process of gathering, modeling, and transforming data with the goal of highlighting useful information, suggesting conclusions, and supporting decision making. _____ has multiple facets and approaches, encompassing diverse techniques under a variety of names, in different business, science, and social science domains.

Data mining is a particular _____ technique that focuses on modeling and knowledge discovery for predictive rather than purely descriptive purposes.

a. Power III
c. 180SearchAssistant

b. 6-3-5 Brainwriting
d. Data analysis

19. _____ is that part of statistical practice concerned with the selection of individual observations intended to yield some knowledge about a population of concern, especially for the purposes of statistical inference. Each observation measures one or more properties (weight, location, etc.) of an observable entity enumerated to distinguish objects or individuals.

a. Richard Buckminster 'Bucky' Fuller
c. AStore

b. Sampling
d. Sports Marketing Group

20. _____ is defined by communication scholars in numerous ways, usually describing participants who are dependent upon one another and have a shared history. Communication channels, the conceptualization of mediums that carry messages from sender to receiver, take two distinct forms: direct and indirect.

Direct channels are obvious and easily recognized by the receiver.

a. Interpersonal communication
c. ACNielsen

b. ADTECH
d. AMAX

21. In economics, business, retail, and accounting, a _____ is the value of money that has been used up to produce something, and hence is not available for use anymore. In economics, a _____ is an alternative that is given up as a result of a decision. In business, the _____ may be one of acquisition, in which case the amount of money expended to acquire it is counted as _____.

a. Fixed costs
c. Variable cost

b. Transaction cost
d. Cost

Chapter 6. Exploratory Designs: In-Depth Interviews and Focus Groups

22. A _____ is a form of qualitative research in which a group of people are asked about their attitude towards a product, service, concept, advertisement, idea, or packaging. Questions are asked in an interactive group setting where participants are free to talk with other group members.

Ernest Dichter originated the idea of having a 'group therapy' for products and this process is what became known as a _____.

    a. Focus group
    b. Logit analysis
    c. Cross tabulation
    d. Marketing research process

23. _____ is a broad label that refers to any individuals or households that use goods and services generated within the economy. The concept of a _____ is used in different contexts, so that the usage and significance of the term may vary.

A _____ is a person who uses any product or service.

    a. 6-3-5 Brainwriting
    b. 180SearchAssistant
    c. Power III
    d. Consumer

24. _____ is the study of when, why, how, where and what people do or do not buy products. It blends elements from psychology, sociology, social psychology, anthropology and economics. It attempts to understand the buyer decision making process, both individually and in groups. It studies characteristics of individual consumers such as demographics and behavioural variables in an attempt to understand people's wants. It also tries to assess influences on the consumer from groups such as family, friends, reference groups, and society in general.

    a. Consumer confidence
    b. Consumer behavior
    c. Communal marketing
    d. Multidimensional scaling

25. _____ in organizations and public policy is both the organizational process of creating and maintaining a plan; and the psychological process of thinking about the activities required to create a desired goal on some scale. As such, it is a fundamental property of intelligent behavior. This thought process is essential to the creation and refinement of a plan, or integration of it with other plans, that is, it combines forecasting of developments with the preparation of scenarios of how to react to them.

    a. 6-3-5 Brainwriting
    b. Power III
    c. 180SearchAssistant
    d. Planning

26. Sampling is the use of a subset of the population to represent the whole population. Probability sampling, or random sampling, is a sampling technique in which the probability of getting any particular sample may be calculated. _____ does not meet this criterion and should be used with caution.

    a. Power III
    b. Snowball sampling
    c. Quota sampling
    d. Nonprobability sampling

27. _____ is a way of expressing knowledge or belief that an event will occur or has occurred. In mathematics the concept has been given an exact meaning in _____ theory, that is used extensively in such areas of study as mathematics, statistics, finance, gambling, science, and philosophy to draw conclusions about the likelihood of potential events and the underlying mechanics of complex systems.

68 *Chapter 6. Exploratory Designs: In-Depth Interviews and Focus Groups*

    a. Probability
    b. Heteroskedastic
    c. Linear regression
    d. Data

28. A _____ is an advance video or DVD copy of a film sent to critics, awards voters, video stores (for their manager and employees), and other film industry professionals, including producers and distributors. Often, each individual _____ is sent out with distinct markings (such as a digital watermark), which allow copies of a _____ to be tracked to their source.

In 2003 the MPAA announced that they would be ceasing distribution of _____s to Academy members, citing fears of piracy.

    a. Screener
    b. Trademark dilution
    c. Madrid system
    d. Geographical indication

29. In social science research, _____ is a technique for developing a research sample where existing study subjects recruit future subjects from among their acquaintances. Thus the sample group appears to grow like a rolling snowball. As the sample builds up, enough data is gathered to be useful for research.

    a. Power III
    b. Snowball sampling
    c. Nonprobability sampling
    d. Quota sampling

30. _____ is the process of making something random; this means:

- Generating a random permutation of a sequence (such as when shuffling cards.)
- Selecting a random sample of a population (important in statistical sampling.)
- Generating random numbers: see Random number generation.
- Transforming a data stream using a scrambler in telecommunications.

_____ is used extensively in the field of gambling (or generally being random.) Imperfect _____ may allow a skilled gambler to have an advantage, so much research has been devoted to effective _____. A classic example of _____ is shuffling playing cards.

_____ is a core principle in the statistical theory of design of experiments.

    a. Statistics
    b. Standard deviation
    c. Sample size
    d. Randomization

31. Consumer market research is a form of applied sociology that concentrates on understanding the behaviours, whims and preferences, of consumers in a market-based economy, and aims to understand the effects and comparative success of marketing campaigns. The field of consumer _____ as a statistical science was pioneered by Arthur Nielsen with the founding of the ACNielsen Company in 1923 .

Thus _____ is the systematic and objective identification, collection, analysis, and dissemination of information for the purpose of assisting management in decision making related to the identification and solution of problems and opportunities in marketing.

Chapter 6. Exploratory Designs: In-Depth Interviews and Focus Groups

a. Focus group
b. Logit analysis
c. Marketing research
d. Marketing research process

32. In economics and sociology, an _____ is any factor (financial or non-financial) that enables or motivates a particular course of action, or counts as a reason for preferring one choice to the alternatives. It is an expectation that encourages people to behave in a certain way. Since human beings are purposeful creatures, the study of _____ structures is central to the study of all economic activity (both in terms of individual decision-making and in terms of co-operation and competition within a larger institutional structure.)

   a. Incentive
   b. ACNielsen
   c. AMAX
   d. ADTECH

33. The _____ is a form of reactivity, The term was coined in 1955 by Henry A. Landsberger when analyzing older experiments from 1924-1932 at the Hawthorne Works (outside Chicago.) Landsberger defined the _____ as:

   - a short-term improvement caused by observing worker performance.

Earlier researchers had concluded the short-term improvement was caused by teamwork when workers saw themselves as part of a study group or team. Others have broadened the definition to mean that people's behavior and performance change following any new or increased attention. Hence, the term _____ no longer has a specific definition.

   a. 180SearchAssistant
   b. 6-3-5 Brainwriting
   c. Power III
   d. Hawthorne effect

34. _____ is a standard point of view or personal prejudice. especially when the tendency interferes with the ability to be impartial, unprejudiced, or objective. The term _____ed is used to describe an action, judgment, or other outcome influenced by a prejudged perspective.

   a. 180SearchAssistant
   b. Power III
   c. 6-3-5 Brainwriting
   d. Bias

35. _____ is a methodology in the social sciences for studying the content of communication. Earl Babbie defines it as 'the study of recorded human communications, such as books, websites, paintings and laws.' It is most commonly used by researchers in the social sciences to analyze recorded transcripts of interviews with participants.

_____ is also considered a scholarly methodology in the humanities by which texts are studied as to authorship, authenticity, of meaning.

   a. 6-3-5 Brainwriting
   b. Content analysis
   c. Power III
   d. 180SearchAssistant

36. In statistics, _____ or estimation error is the error caused by observing a sample instead of the whole population.

An estimate of a quantity of interest, such as an average or percentage, will generally be subject to sample-to-sample variation. These variations in the possible sample values of a statistic can theoretically be expressed as _____s, although in practice the exact _____ is typically unknown.

a. Varimax rotation
b. Power III
c. Sampling error
d. Two-tailed test

37. A _____ is a subgroup of people or organizations sharing one or more characteristics that cause them to have similar product and/or service needs. A true _____ meets all of the following criteria: it is distinct from other segments (different segments have different needs), it is homogeneous within the segment (exhibits common needs); it responds similarly to a market stimulus, and it can be reached by a market intervention. The term is also used when consumers with identical product and/or service needs are divided up into groups so they can be charged different amounts.

a. Production orientation
b. Market segment
c. Commercial planning
d. Customer insight

38. In descriptive statistics, the _____ is the length of the smallest interval which contains all the data. It is calculated by subtracting the smallest observation (sample minimum) from the greatest (sample maximum) and provides an indication of statistical dispersion.

It is measured in the same units as the data.

a. Personalization
b. Range
c. Just-In-Case
d. Japan Advertising Photographers' Association

39. In statistics, an _____ is a term in a statistical model added when the effect of two or more variables is not simply additive. Such a term reflects that the effect of one variable depends on the values of one or more other variables.

Thus, for a response Y and two variables x_1 and x_2 an additive model would be:

$$Y = ax_1 + bx_2 + \text{error}$$

In contrast to this,

$$Y = ax_1 + bx_2 + c(x_1 \times x_2) + \text{error},$$

is an example of a model with an _____ between variables x_1 and x_2 ('error' refers to the random variable whose value by which y differs from the expected value of y.)

a. ADTECH
b. AMAX
c. ACNielsen
d. Interaction

40. _____ refers to the evolving trend in marketing whereby marketing has moved from a transaction-based effort to a conversation. The definition of _____ comes from John Deighton at Harvard, who says _____ is the ability to address the customer, remember what the customer says and address the customer again in a way that illustrates that we remember what the customer has told us (Deighton 1996.) _____ is not synonymous with online marketing, although _____ processes are facilitated by internet technology.

a. Outsourcing relationship management
b. European Information Technology Observatory
c. Interactive marketing
d. InfoNU

Chapter 6. Exploratory Designs: In-Depth Interviews and Focus Groups

41. An _____ is one type of focus group, and is a sub-set of online research methods.

A moderator invites prescreened, qualified respondents who represent the target of interest to log on to conferencing software at a pre-arranged time and to take part in an _____. Some researchers will offer incentives for participating but this raises a number of ethical questions.

   a. Engagement
   b. Intangibility
   c. Automated surveys
   d. Online focus group

42. _____ or _____ data refers to selected population characteristics as used in government, marketing or opinion research, or the _____ profiles used in such research. Note the distinction from the term 'demography' Commonly-used _____ include race, age, income, disabilities, mobility (in terms of travel time to work or number of vehicles available), educational attainment, home ownership, employment status, and even location.
   a. AStore
   b. Albert Einstein
   c. African Americans
   d. Demographic

43. _____ are a class of semi-structured projective techniques. _____ typically provide respondents with beginnings of sentences, referred to as 'stems,' and respondents then complete the sentences in ways that are meaningful to them. The responses are believed to provide indications of attitudes, beliefs, motivations, or other mental states.
   a. Response rate
   b. Reference value
   c. Power III
   d. Sentence completion tests

44. _____ is a common word game involving an exchange of words that are associated together.

Once an original word has been chosen, usually randomly or arbitrarily, a player will find a word that they associate with it and make it known to all the players, usually by saying it aloud or writing it down as the next item on a list of words so far used. The next player must then do the same with this previous word.

   a. Power III
   b. 180SearchAssistant
   c. 6-3-5 Brainwriting
   d. Word association

Chapter 7. Descriptive Research Designs: Survey Methods and Errors

1. _____ is defined by the American _____ Association as the activity, set of institutions, and processes for creating, communicating, delivering, and exchanging offerings that have value for customers, clients, partners, and society at large. The term developed from the original meaning which referred literally to going to market, as in shopping, or going to a market to sell goods or services.

_____ practice tends to be seen as a creative industry, which includes advertising, distribution and selling.

   a. Customer acquisition management   b. Product naming
   c. Marketing   d. Marketing myopia

2. Consumer market research is a form of applied sociology that concentrates on understanding the behaviours, whims and preferences, of consumers in a market-based economy, and aims to understand the effects and comparative success of marketing campaigns. The field of consumer _____ as a statistical science was pioneered by Arthur Nielsen with the founding of the ACNielsen Company in 1923 .

Thus _____ is the systematic and objective identification, collection, analysis, and dissemination of information for the purpose of assisting management in decision making related to the identification and solution of problems and opportunities in marketing.

   a. Logit analysis   b. Marketing research process
   c. Focus group   d. Marketing research

3. _____ describes data and characteristics about the population or phenomenon being studied. _____ answers the questions who, what, where, when and how.

Although the data description is factual, accurate and systematic, the research cannot describe what caused a situation.

   a. Power III   b. Two-tailed test
   c. Sampling error   d. Descriptive research

4. _____ a research method involving the use of questionnaires and/or statistical surveys to gather data about people and their thoughts and behaviours.
   a. T-test   b. Z-test
   c. Control chart   d. Survey research

5. _____ is the provision of service to customers before, during and after a purchase.

According to Turban et al., '_____ is a series of activities designed to enhance the level of customer satisfaction - that is, the feeling that a product or service has met the customer expectation.'

Its importance varies by product, industry and customer.

   a. COPC Inc.   b. Customer experience
   c. Facing   d. Customer service

Chapter 7. Descriptive Research Designs: Survey Methods and Errors   73

6. A number of different _____s are indicated below.

- Randomized controlled trial
    - Double-blind randomized trial
    - Single-blind randomized trial
    - Non-blind trial
- Nonrandomized trial (quasi-experiment)
    - Interrupted time series design (measures on a sample or a series of samples from the same population are obtained several times before and after a manipulated event or a naturally occurring event) - considered a type of quasi-experiment

- Cohort study
    - Prospective cohort
    - Retrospective cohort
    - Time series study
- Case-control study
    - Nested case-control study
- Cross-sectional study
    - Community survey (a type of cross-sectional study)

When choosing a _____, many factors must be taken into account. Different types of studies are subject to different types of bias. For example, recall bias is likely to occur in cross-sectional or case-control studies where subjects are asked to recall exposure to risk factors.

a. Study design
c. Longitudinal studies
b. Power III
d. 180SearchAssistant

7. _____ is an advertisement in which a particular product specifically mentions a competitor by name for the express purpose of showing why the competitor is inferior to the product naming it.

This should not be confused with parody advertisements, where a fictional product is being advertised for the purpose of poking fun at the particular advertisement, nor should it be confused with the use of a coined brand name for the purpose of comparing the product without actually naming an actual competitor. ('Wikipedia tastes better and is less filling than the Encyclopedia Galactica.')

In the 1980s, during what has been referred to as the cola wars, soft-drink manufacturer Pepsi ran a series of advertisements where people, caught on hidden camera, in a blind taste test, chose Pepsi over rival Coca-Cola.

a. Heavy-up
c. GL-70
b. Cost per conversion
d. Comparative advertising

8. A personal and cultural _____ is a relative ethic _____, an assumption upon which implementation can be extrapolated. A _____ system is a set of consistent _____s and measures that is soo not true. A principle _____ is a foundation upon which other _____s and measures of integrity are based.

a. Supreme Court of the United States
b. Package-on-Package
c. Perceptual maps
d. Value

9. _____ is a term for unprocessed data, it is also known as primary data. It is a relative term _____ can be input to a computer program or used in manual analysis procedures such as gathering statistics from a survey.
   a. Chief marketing officer
   b. Shoppers Food ' Pharmacy
   c. Product manager
   d. Raw data

10. A _____ attribute is one that exists in a range of magnitudes, and can therefore be measured. Measurements of any particular _____ property are expressed as a specific quantity, referred to as a unit, multiplied by a number. Examples of physical quantities are distance, mass, and time.
   a. Lifestyle city
   b. BeyondROI
   c. Dolly Dimples
   d. Quantitative

11. A _____ is a research instrument consisting of a series of questions and other prompts for the purpose of gathering information from respondents. Although they are often designed for statistical analysis of the responses, this is not always the case. The _____ was invented by Sir Francis Galton.
   a. Mystery shoppers
   b. Mystery shopping
   c. Market research
   d. Questionnaire

12. _____ refer to a collection of facts usually collected as the result of experience, observation or experiment or a set of premises. This may consist of numbers, words particularly as measurements or observations of a set of variables. _____ are often viewed as a lowest level of abstraction from which information and knowledge are derived.
   a. Mean
   b. Pearson product-moment correlation coefficient
   c. Sample size
   d. Data

13. _____ is a term used to describe a process of preparing and collecting data - for example as part of a process improvement or similar project.

_____ usually takes place early on in an improvement project, and is often formalised through a _____ Plan which often contains the following activity.

1. Pre collection activity - Agree goals, target data, definitions, methods
2. Collection - _____
3. Present Findings - usually involves some form of sorting analysis and/or presentation.

A formal _____ process is necessary as it ensures that data gathered is both defined and accurate and that subsequent decisions based on arguments embodied in the findings are valid . The process provides both a baseline from which to measure from and in certain cases a target on what to improve. Types of _____ 1-By mail questionnaires 2-By personal interview

- Six sigma
- Sampling (statistics)

Chapter 7. Descriptive Research Designs: Survey Methods and Errors

    a. 6-3-5 Brainwriting   b. Power III
    c. 180SearchAssistant   d. Data collection

14. _____ is a contract between two parties, one being the employer and the other being the employee. An employee may be defined as: 'A person in the service of another under any contract of hire, express or implied, oral or written, where the employer has the power or right to control and direct the employee in the material details of how the work is to be performed.' Black's Law Dictionary page 471 (5th ed. 1979.)
    a. ADTECH   b. AMAX
    c. ACNielsen   d. Employment

15. _____ is a computer program used for statistical analysis.

_____ (originally, Statistical Package for the Social Sciences) was released in its first version in 1968 after being founded by Norman Nie and C. Hadlai Hull. Nie was then a political science postgraduate at Stanford University, and now Research Professor in the Department of Political Science at Stanford and Professor Emeritus of Political Science at the University of Chicago.

    a. 180SearchAssistant   b. SPSS
    c. 6-3-5 Brainwriting   d. Power III

16. _____ is a process of gathering, modeling, and transforming data with the goal of highlighting useful information, suggesting conclusions, and supporting decision making. _____ has multiple facets and approaches, encompassing diverse techniques under a variety of names, in different business, science, and social science domains.

Data mining is a particular _____ technique that focuses on modeling and knowledge discovery for predictive rather than purely descriptive purposes.

    a. Power III   b. 180SearchAssistant
    c. 6-3-5 Brainwriting   d. Data analysis

17. The _____ of a statistical sample is the number of observations that constitute it. It is typically denoted n, a positive integer (natural number.)

Typically, all else being equal, a larger _____ leads to increased precision in estimates of various properties of the population.

    a. Sample size   b. Data
    c. Heteroskedastic   d. Frequency distribution

18. _____ is a standard point of view or personal prejudice. especially when the tendency interferes with the ability to be impartial, unprejudiced, or objective. The term _____ed is used to describe an action, judgment, or other outcome influenced by a prejudged perspective.
    a. Power III   b. 180SearchAssistant
    c. 6-3-5 Brainwriting   d. Bias

19. _____ is either an activity of a living being (such as a human), consisting of receiving knowledge of the outside world through the senses, or the recording of data using scientific instruments. The term may also refer to any datum collected during this activity.

The scientific method requires _____s of nature to formulate and test hypotheses.

   a. ADTECH
   c. AMAX
   b. ACNielsen
   d. Observation

20. _____ is that part of statistical practice concerned with the selection of individual observations intended to yield some knowledge about a population of concern, especially for the purposes of statistical inference. Each observation measures one or more properties (weight, location, etc.) of an observable entity enumerated to distinguish objects or individuals.
   a. Sports Marketing Group
   c. AStore
   b. Richard Buckminster 'Bucky' Fuller
   d. Sampling

21. In statistics, _____ or estimation error is the error caused by observing a sample instead of the whole population.

An estimate of a quantity of interest, such as an average or percentage, will generally be subject to sample-to-sample variation. These variations in the possible sample values of a statistic can theoretically be expressed as _____s, although in practice the exact _____ is typically unknown.

   a. Power III
   c. Sampling error
   b. Two-tailed test
   d. Varimax rotation

22. _____s are biases in measurement which lead to the situation where the mean of many separate measurements differs significantly from the actual value of the measured attribute. All measurements are prone to _____s, often of several different types. Sources of _____ may be imperfect calibration of measurement instruments, changes in the environment which interfere with the measurement process and sometimes imperfect methods of observation can be either zero error or percentage error.
   a. Power III
   c. 180SearchAssistant
   b. Systematic bias
   d. Systematic error

23. In statistics, a _____ is an interval estimate of a population parameter. Instead of estimating the parameter by a single value, an interval likely to include the parameter is given. Thus, _____s are used to indicate the reliability of an estimate.
   a. Confidence interval
   c. Linear regression
   b. Sample mean
   d. T-test

24. _____ is a type of cognitive bias which can affect the results of a statistical survey if respondents answer questions in the way they think the questioner wants them to answer rather than according to their true beliefs. This may occur if the questioner is obviously angling for a particular answer (as in push polling) or if the respondent wishes to please the questioner by answering what appears to be the 'morally right' answer. An example of the latter might be if a woman surveys a man on his attitudes to domestic violence, or someone who obviously cares about the environment asks people how much they value a wilderness area.

a. Response bias
b. 180SearchAssistant
c. Von Restorff effect
d. Power III

25. _____ is the process of extracting hidden patterns from data. As more data is gathered, with the amount of data doubling every three years, _____ is becoming an increasingly important tool to transform this data into information. It is commonly used in a wide range of profiling practices, such as marketing, surveillance, fraud detection and scientific discovery.
a. Structure mining
b. Power III
c. 180SearchAssistant
d. Data mining

26. _____ is the difference between a measured value of quantity and its true value. In statistics, an error is not a 'mistake'. Variability is an inherent part of things being measured and of the measurement process.
a. ADTECH
b. Observational error
c. ACNielsen
d. AMAX

27. _____s are used in open sentences. For instance, in the formula x + 1 = 5, x is a _____ which represents an 'unknown' number. _____s are often represented by letters of the Roman alphabet, or those of other alphabets, such as Greek, and use other special symbols.
a. Book of business
b. Personalization
c. Quantitative
d. Variable

28. In psychology, philosophy, and the cognitive sciences, _____ is the process of attaining awareness or understanding of sensory information. It is a task far more complex than was imagined in the 1950s and 1960s, when it was predicted that building perceiving machines would take about a decade, a goal which is still very far from fruition. The word _____ comes from the Latin words _____, percepio, meaning 'receiving, collecting, action of taking possession, apprehension with the mind or senses.'

_____ is one of the oldest fields in psychology.

a. Groupthink
b. 180SearchAssistant
c. Power III
d. Perception

29. _____ is a type of research conducted because a problem has not been clearly defined. _____ helps determine the best research design, data collection method and selection of subjects. Given its fundamental nature, _____ often concludes that a perceived problem does not actually exist.
a. Intent scale translation
b. IDDEA
c. ACNielsen
d. Exploratory research

30. _____ is a telephone surveying technique in which the interviewer follows a script provided by a software application. The software is able to customize the flow of the questionnaire based on the answers provided, as well as information already known about the participant.

Chapter 7. Descriptive Research Designs: Survey Methods and Errors

CATI may function in the following manner

- A computerized questionnaire is administered to respondents over the telephone.
- The interviewer sits in front of a computer screen
- Upon command, the computer dials the telephone number to be called.
- When contact is made, the interviewer reads the questions posed on the computer screen and records the respondent's answers directly into the computer.
- Interim and update reports can be compiled instantaneously, as the data are being collected.
- CATI software has built-in logic, which also enhances data accuracy.
- The program will personalize questions and control for logically incorrect answers, such as percentage answers that do not add up to 100 percent.
- The software has built-in branching logic, which will skip questions that are not applicable or will probe for more detail when warranted.

  a. Power III
  b. 180SearchAssistant
  c. 6-3-5 Brainwriting
  d. Computer-assisted telephone interviewing

31. A _____ is an error that occurs when a person performs an action on an object that is not the object intended. This error can be very disorienting and usually causes a brief loss of situation awareness or automation surprise if noticed right away. But much worse, if it goes unnoticed, it could cause more serious problems.
  a. Power III
  b. Description error
  c. Motivation
  d. 180SearchAssistant

32. A _____ is an explicit set of requirements to be satisfied by a material, product, or service.

In engineering, manufacturing, and business, it is vital for suppliers, purchasers, and users of materials, products, or services to understand and agree upon all requirements. A _____ is a type of a standard which is often referenced by a contract or procurement document.

  a. Specification
  b. Product optimization
  c. Product development
  d. New product development

33. In economics, business, retail, and accounting, a _____ is the value of money that has been used up to produce something, and hence is not available for use anymore. In economics, a _____ is an alternative that is given up as a result of a decision. In business, the _____ may be one of acquisition, in which case the amount of money expended to acquire it is counted as _____.
  a. Transaction cost
  b. Cost
  c. Variable cost
  d. Fixed costs

34. The _____ is a professional association for marketers. As of 2008 it had approximately 40,000 members. There are collegiate chapters on 250 campuses.

a. American Marketing Association
b. ACNielsen
c. AMAX
d. ADTECH

35. _____ is a broad label that refers to any individuals or households that use goods and services generated within the economy. The concept of a _____ is used in different contexts, so that the usage and significance of the term may vary.

A _____ is a person who uses any product or service.

a. 180SearchAssistant
b. Power III
c. 6-3-5 Brainwriting
d. Consumer

36. _____ is a form of government regulation which protects the interests of consumers. For example, a government may require businesses to disclose detailed information about products--particularly in areas where safety or public health is an issue, such as food. _____ is linked to the idea of consumer rights (that consumers have various rights as consumers), and to the formation of consumer organizations which help consumers make better choices in the marketplace.

a. Sound trademark
b. Consumer Protection
c. Trademark dilution
d. Federal Bureau of Investigation

37. _____ is a sub-discipline and type of marketing. There are two main definitional characteristics which distinguish it from other types of marketing. The first is that it attempts to send its messages directly to consumers, without the use of intervening media.

a. Direct Marketing Associations
b. Power III
c. Direct Marketing
d. Database marketing

38. _____ are national trade organizations that seek to advance all forms of direct marketing.

23 direct marketing trade associations from five continents established an International Federation of _____. Founded in 1989, the IFDirect Marketing Associations was established to develop firm lines of communications between direct marketers around the world, and is dedicated to improving the practice and communicating the value of direct marketing; and to promoting the highest standards for ethical conduct and effective self-regulation of the direct marketing community.

a. Database marketing
b. Direct marketing
c. Power III
d. Direct Marketing Associations

39. _____ is a branch of philosophy which seeks to address questions about morality, such as how a moral outcome can be achieved in a specific situation (applied _____), how moral values should be determined (normative _____), what moral values people actually abide by (descriptive _____), what the fundamental semantic, ontological, and epistemic nature of _____ or morality is (meta-_____), and how moral capacity or moral agency develops and what its nature is (moral psychology.)

Socrates was one of the first Greek philosophers to encourage both scholars and the common citizen to turn their attention from the outside world to the condition of man. In this view, Knowledge having a bearing on human life was placed highest, all other knowledge being secondary.

a. ACNielsen
b. Ethics
c. ADTECH
d. AMAX

40. _____ is the ability of an individual or group to seclude themselves or information about themselves and thereby reveal themselves selectively. The boundaries and content of what is considered private differ among cultures and individuals, but share basic common themes. _____ is sometimes related to anonymity, the wish to remain unnoticed or unidentified in the public realm.
   a. Privacy
   b. Power III
   c. 6-3-5 Brainwriting
   d. 180SearchAssistant

41. _____ is a market research industry term, meaning 'selling under the guise of research'. This behavior occurs when a product marketer falsely pretends to be a market researcher conducting a survey, when in reality they are simply trying to sell the product in question.

Generally considered unethical, this tactic is prohibited or strongly disapproved of by trade groups, such as the UK Market Research Society MRS, CASRO and MRA, for their member research companies.

   a. Sugging
   b. Perishability
   c. Brand parity
   d. Demonstrator model

42. _____ is a method of direct marketing in which a salesperson solicits to prospective customers to buy products or services, either over the phone or through a subsequent face to face or Web conferencing appointment scheduled during the call.

_____ can also include recorded sales pitches programmed to be played over the phone via automatic dialing. _____ has come under fire in recent years, being viewed as an annoyance by many.

   a. Phishing
   b. Joe job
   c. Directory Harvest Attack
   d. Telemarketing

43. Procter is a surname, and may also refer to:

   - Bryan Waller Procter (pseud. Barry Cornwall), English poet
   - Goodwin Procter, American law firm
   - _____, consumer products multinational

   a. Flyer
   b. Black PRies
   c. Convergent
   d. Procter ' Gamble

44. _____ are used to collect information and gain feedback via the telephone and the internet. _____ are used for customer research purposes by call centres for customer relationship management and performance management purposes. They are also used for political polling, market research and job satisfaction surveying.
   a. Individual branding
   b. Engagement
   c. Automated surveys
   d. Intangibility

Chapter 7. Descriptive Research Designs: Survey Methods and Errors

45. A _____ is a psychometric scale commonly used in questionnaires, and is the most widely used scale in survey research. When responding to a Likert questionnaire item, respondents specify their level of agreement to a statement. The scale is named after its inventor, psychologist Rensis Likert.
   a. Power III
   b. Factor analysis
   c. Likert scale
   d. Semantic differential

46. _____ are used to collect quantitative information about items in a population. Surveys of human populations and institutions are common in political polling and government, health, social science and marketing research. A survey may focus on opinions or factual information depending on its purpose, and many surveys involve administering questions to individuals.
   a. Gross Margin Return on Inventory Investment
   b. Convergent
   c. BeyondROI
   d. Statistical surveys

47. A _____ is a structured collection of records or data that is stored in a computer system. The structure is achieved by organizing the data according to a _____ model. The model in most common use today is the relational model.
   a. 6-3-5 Brainwriting
   b. 180SearchAssistant
   c. Power III
   d. Database

48. In engineering and manufacturing, _____ is involved in developing systems to ensure products or services are designed and produced to meet or exceed customer requirements or SLA's. Genetic algorithms are search techniques, used in computing to find exact or approximate solutions to optimization and search problems.

Alternative _____ procedures can be applied on a process to test statistically the null hypothesis, that the process is in control, against the alternative, that the process is out of control.

   a. Quality control
   b. 180SearchAssistant
   c. Power III
   d. 6-3-5 Brainwriting

49. The _____ is the number of new cases per unit of person-time at risk. In the same example as above, the _____ is 14 cases per 1000 person-years, because the incidence proportion (28 per 1,000) is divided by the number of years (two.) Using person-time rather than just time handles situations where the amount of observation time differs between people, or when the population at risk varies with time.
   a. ACNielsen
   b. AMAX
   c. ADTECH
   d. Incidence rate

50. In economics and sociology, an _____ is any factor (financial or non-financial) that enables or motivates a particular course of action, or counts as a reason for preferring one choice to the alternatives. It is an expectation that encourages people to behave in a certain way. Since human beings are purposeful creatures, the study of _____ structures is central to the study of all economic activity (both in terms of individual decision-making and in terms of co-operation and competition within a larger institutional structure.)
   a. ACNielsen
   b. AMAX
   c. Incentive
   d. ADTECH

51. _____ is a list for goods and materials held available in stock by a business. It is also used for a list of the contents of a household and for a list for testamentary purposes of the possessions of someone who has died. In accounting _____ is considered an asset.

a. ACNielsen
b. Ending Inventory
c. Inventory
d. ADTECH

52. In probability theory and statistics, _____ indicates the strength and direction of a linear relationship between two random variables. That is in contrast with the usage of the term in colloquial speech, denoting any relationship, not necessarily linear. In general statistical usage, _____ or co-relation refers to the departure of two random variables from independence.
   a. Correlation
   b. Frequency distribution
   c. Probability
   d. Mean

Chapter 8. Observation Techniques, Experiments, and Test Markets 83

1. _____s are used in open sentences. For instance, in the formula x + 1 = 5, x is a _____ which represents an 'unknown' number. _____s are often represented by letters of the Roman alphabet, or those of other alphabets, such as Greek, and use other special symbols.
   a. Personalization
   b. Quantitative
   c. Book of business
   d. Variable

2. A number of different _____s are indicated below.

   - Randomized controlled trial
     - Double-blind randomized trial
     - Single-blind randomized trial
     - Non-blind trial
   - Nonrandomized trial (quasi-experiment)
     - Interrupted time series design (measures on a sample or a series of samples from the same population are obtained several times before and after a manipulated event or a naturally occurring event) - considered a type of quasi-experiment

   - Cohort study
     - Prospective cohort
     - Retrospective cohort
     - Time series study
   - Case-control study
     - Nested case-control study
   - Cross-sectional study
     - Community survey (a type of cross-sectional study)

   When choosing a _____, many factors must be taken into account. Different types of studies are subject to different types of bias. For example, recall bias is likely to occur in cross-sectional or case-control studies where subjects are asked to recall exposure to risk factors.

   a. Longitudinal studies
   b. Power III
   c. 180SearchAssistant
   d. Study design

3. A _____ applies the scientific method to experimentally examine an intervention in the real world (or as many experimental economists like to say, naturally-occurring environments) rather than in the laboratory. _____s, like lab experiments, generally randomize subjects (or other sampling units) into treatment and control groups and compare outcomes between these groups. Clinical trials of pharmaceuticals are one example of _____s.
   a. 180SearchAssistant
   b. Power III
   c. Response variable
   d. Field experiment

4. _____ is defined by the American _____ Association as the activity, set of institutions, and processes for creating, communicating, delivering, and exchanging offerings that have value for customers, clients, partners, and society at large. The term developed from the original meaning which referred literally to going to market, as in shopping, or going to a market to sell goods or services.

   _____ practice tends to be seen as a creative industry, which includes advertising, distribution and selling.

Chapter 8. Observation Techniques, Experiments, and Test Markets

a. Product naming
b. Marketing myopia
c. Customer acquisition management
d. Marketing

5. _____ is either an activity of a living being (such as a human), consisting of receiving knowledge of the outside world through the senses, or the recording of data using scientific instruments. The term may also refer to any datum collected during this activity.

The scientific method requires _____ s of nature to formulate and test hypotheses.

a. ADTECH
b. ACNielsen
c. AMAX
d. Observation

6. A _____, in the field of business and marketing, is a geographic region or demographic group used to gauge the viability of a product or service in the mass market prior to a wide scale roll-out. The criteria used to judge the acceptability of a _____ region or group include:

1. a population that is demographically similar to the proposed target market; and
2. relative isolation from densely populated media markets so that advertising to the test audience can be efficient and economical.

The _____ ideally aims to duplicate 'everything' - promotion and distribution as well as `product' - on a smaller scale. The technique replicates, typically in one area, what is planned to occur in a national launch; and the results are very carefully monitored, so that they can be extrapolated to projected national results. The `area' may be any one of the following:

- Television area
- Test town
- Residential neighborhood
- Test site

A number of decisions have to be taken about any _____:

- Which _____?
- What is to be tested?
- How long a test?
- What are the success criteria?

The simple go or no-go decision, together with the related reduction of risk, is normally the main justification for the expense of _____ s. At the same time, however, such _____ s can be used to test specific elements of a new product's marketing mix; possibly the version of the product itself, the promotional message and media spend, the distribution channels and the price.

a. 180SearchAssistant
b. Test market
c. Preadolescence
d. Power III

Chapter 8. Observation Techniques, Experiments, and Test Markets

7. A personal and cultural _____ is a relative ethic _____, an assumption upon which implementation can be extrapolated. A _____ system is a set of consistent _____s and measures that is soo not true. A principle _____ is a foundation upon which other _____s and measures of integrity are based.
   a. Supreme Court of the United States
   b. Package-on-Package
   c. Perceptual maps
   d. Value

8. _____ is a global marketing research firm, with worldwide headquarters in New York City. Regional headquarters for North America are located in Schaumburg, IL. As of 2008, its the part of The Nielsen Company.
   a. ACNielsen
   b. Alloy Entertainment
   c. E-Detailing
   d. InfoNU

9. _____ refer to a collection of facts usually collected as the result of experience, observation or experiment or a set of premises. This may consist of numbers, words particularly as measurements or observations of a set of variables. _____ are often viewed as a lowest level of abstraction from which information and knowledge are derived.
   a. Data
   b. Mean
   c. Pearson product-moment correlation coefficient
   d. Sample size

10. _____ is a branch of philosophy which seeks to address questions about morality, such as how a moral outcome can be achieved in a specific situation (applied _____), how moral values should be determined (normative _____), what moral values people actually abide by (descriptive _____), what the fundamental semantic, ontological, and epistemic nature of _____ or morality is (meta-_____), and how moral capacity or moral agency develops and what its nature is (moral psychology.)

Socrates was one of the first Greek philosophers to encourage both scholars and the common citizen to turn their attention from the outside world to the condition of man. In this view, Knowledge having a bearing on human life was placed highest, all other knowledge being secondary.

   a. ADTECH
   b. AMAX
   c. ACNielsen
   d. Ethics

11. Mystery shopping or Mystery Consumer is a tool used by market research companies to measure quality of retail service or gather specific information about products and services. _____ posing as normal customers perform specific tasks-- such as purchasing a product, asking questions, registering complaints or behaving in a certain way - and then provide detailed reports or feedback about their experiences.

Mystery shopping began in the 1940s as a way to measure employee integrity.

   a. Market research
   b. Questionnaire
   c. Mystery shopping
   d. Mystery shoppers

12. _____ is the ability of an individual or group to seclude themselves or information about themselves and thereby reveal themselves selectively. The boundaries and content of what is considered private differ among cultures and individuals, but share basic common themes. _____ is sometimes related to anonymity, the wish to remain unnoticed or unidentified in the public realm.

Chapter 8. Observation Techniques, Experiments, and Test Markets

a. Power III
b. 180SearchAssistant
c. 6-3-5 Brainwriting
d. Privacy

13. A _____ is a tool used to measure the viewing habits of TV and cable audiences.

The _____ is a 'box', about the size of a paperback book. The box is hooked up to each television set and is accompanied by a remote control unit.

a. 180SearchAssistant
b. Power III
c. 6-3-5 Brainwriting
d. People Meter

14. _____ is the process of measuring either the point of gaze ('where we are looking') or the motion of an eye relative to the head. An eye tracker is a device for measuring eye positions and eye movements. Eye trackers are used in research on the visual system, in psychology, in cognitive linguistics and in product design.

a. AMAX
b. ADTECH
c. Eye tracking
d. ACNielsen

15. _____ psychogalvanic reflex is a method of measuring the electrical resistance of the skin. There has been a long history of electrodermal activity research, most of it dealing with spontaneous fluctuations. Most investigators accept the phenomenon without understanding exactly what it means.

a. 6-3-5 Brainwriting
b. Galvanic skin response
c. Power III
d. 180SearchAssistant

16. In economics, business, retail, and accounting, a _____ is the value of money that has been used up to produce something, and hence is not available for use anymore. In economics, a _____ is an alternative that is given up as a result of a decision. In business, the _____ may be one of acquisition, in which case the amount of money expended to acquire it is counted as _____.

a. Transaction cost
b. Fixed costs
c. Variable cost
d. Cost

17. The _____ is a professional association for marketers. As of 2008 it had approximately 40,000 members. There are collegiate chapters on 250 campuses.

a. AMAX
b. ADTECH
c. ACNielsen
d. American Marketing Association

18. Consumer market research is a form of applied sociology that concentrates on understanding the behaviours, whims and preferences, of consumers in a market-based economy, and aims to understand the effects and comparative success of marketing campaigns. The field of consumer _____ as a statistical science was pioneered by Arthur Nielsen with the founding of the ACNielsen Company in 1923.

Thus _____ is the systematic and objective identification, collection, analysis, and dissemination of information for the purpose of assisting management in decision making related to the identification and solution of problems and opportunities in marketing.

a. Focus group
c. Logit analysis
b. Marketing research process
d. Marketing Research

19. Human beings are also considered to be _____ because they have the ability to change raw materials into valuable _____. The term Human _____ can also be defined as the skills, energies, talents, abilities and knowledge that are used for the production of goods or the rendering of services. While taking into account human beings as _____, the following things have to be kept in mind:

- The size of the population
- The capabilities of the individuals in that population

Many _____ cannot be consumed in their original form. They have to be processed in order to change them into more usable commodities.

a. Power III
c. 6-3-5 Brainwriting
b. Resources
d. 180SearchAssistant

20. The terms '_____' and 'independent variable' are used in similar but subtly different ways in mathematics and statistics as part of the standard terminology in those subjects. They are used to distinguish between two types of quantities being considered, separating them into those available at the start of a process and those being created by it, where the latter (_____s) are dependent on the former (independent variables.)

In traditional calculus, a function is defined as a relation between two terms called variables because their values vary.

a. Dependent variable
c. 180SearchAssistant
b. Field experiment
d. Power III

21. _____ are variables other than the independent variable that may bear any effect on the behavior of the subject being studied.

_____ are often classified into three main types:

1. Subject variables, which are the characteristics of the individuals being studied that might affect their actions. These variables include age, gender, health status, mood, background, etc.
2. Experimental variables are characteristics of the persons conducting the experiment which might influence how a person behaves. Gender, the presence of racial discrimination, language, or other factors may qualify as such variables.
3. Situational variables are features of the environment in which the study or research was conducted, which have a bearing on the outcome of the experiment in a negative way. Included are the air temperature, level of activity, lighting, and the time of day.

There are two strategies of controlling _____. Either a potentially influential variable is kept the same for all subjects in the research, or they balance the variables in a group.

Take for example an experiment, in which a salesperson sells clothing on a door-to-door basis.

a. AMAX
b. ADTECH
c. ACNielsen
d. Extraneous variables

22. _____ is the process of making something random; this means:

- Generating a random permutation of a sequence (such as when shuffling cards.)
- Selecting a random sample of a population (important in statistical sampling.)
- Generating random numbers: see Random number generation.
- Transforming a data stream using a scrambler in telecommunications.

_____ is used extensively in the field of gambling (or generally being random.) Imperfect _____ may allow a skilled gambler to have an advantage, so much research has been devoted to effective _____. A classic example of _____ is shuffling playing cards.

_____ is a core principle in the statistical theory of design of experiments.

a. Standard deviation
b. Sample size
c. Randomization
d. Statistics

23. _____ is the validity of (causal) inferences in scientific studies, usually based on experiments as experimental validity .

Inferences are said to possess _____ if a causal relation between two variables is properly demonstrated . A causal inference may be based on a relation when three criteria are satisfied:

1. the 'cause' precedes the 'effect' in time (temporal precedence),
2. the 'cause' and the 'effect' are related (covariation), and
3. there are no plausible alternative explanations for the observed covariation (nonspuriousness) .

In scientific experimental settings, researchers often manipulate a variable (the independent variable) to see what effect it has on a second variable (the dependent variable) For example, a researcher might, for different experimental groups, manipulate the dosage of a particular drug between groups to see what effect it has on health. In this example, the researcher wants to make a causal inference, namely, that different doses of the drug may be held responsible for observed changes or differences.

a. ACNielsen
b. AMAX
c. ADTECH
d. Internal validity

Chapter 8. Observation Techniques, Experiments, and Test Markets

24. In social science and psychometrics, _____ refers to whether a scale measures or correlates with a theorized psychological construct (such as 'fluid intelligence'.) It is related to the theoretical ideas behind the personality trait under consideration; a non-existent concept in the physical sense may be suggested as a method of organising how personality can be viewed. The unobservable idea of a unidimensional easier-to-harder dimension must be 'constructed' in the words of human language and graphics.
    a. Discriminant validity
    b. Predictive validity
    c. Construct validity
    d. Criterion validity

25. _____ is a standard point of view or personal prejudice. especially when the tendency interferes with the ability to be impartial, unprejudiced, or objective. The term _____ed is used to describe an action, judgment, or other outcome influenced by a prejudged perspective.
    a. Power III
    b. 6-3-5 Brainwriting
    c. 180SearchAssistant
    d. Bias

26. In economics, an externality or spillover of an economic transaction is an impact on a party that is not directly involved in the transaction. In such a case, prices do not reflect the full costs or benefits in production or consumption of a product or service. A positive impact is called an _____ benefit, while a negative impact is called an _____ cost.
    a. AMAX
    b. ADTECH
    c. ACNielsen
    d. External

27. _____ is the validity of generalized (causal) inferences in scientific studies, usually based on experiments as experimental validity.

Inferences about cause-effect relationships based on a specific scientific study are said to possess _____ if they may be generalized from the unique and idiosyncratic settings, procedures and participants to other populations and conditions Causal inferences said to possess high degrees of _____ can reasonably be expected to apply (a) to the target population of the study (i.e. from which the sample was drawn) (also referred to as population validity), and (b) to the universe of other populations (e.g. across time and space.)

The most common loss of _____ comes from the fact that experiments using human participants often employ small samples obtained from a single geographic location or with idiosyncratic features (e.g. volunteers.)

    a. ADTECH
    b. ACNielsen
    c. AMAX
    d. External validity

28. _____ is a distortion of evidence or data that arises from the way that the data are collected. It is sometimes referred to as the selection effect. The term _____ most often refers to the distortion of a statistical analysis, due to the method of collecting samples.
    a. Systematic sampling
    b. Selection bias
    c. 180SearchAssistant
    d. Power III

29. _____ is a computer program used for statistical analysis.

_____ (originally, Statistical Package for the Social Sciences) was released in its first version in 1968 after being founded by Norman Nie and C. Hadlai Hull. Nie was then a political science postgraduate at Stanford University, and now Research Professor in the Department of Political Science at Stanford and Professor Emeritus of Political Science at the University of Chicago.

a. Power III
b. SPSS
c. 6-3-5 Brainwriting
d. 180SearchAssistant

30. _____ is a process of gathering, modeling, and transforming data with the goal of highlighting useful information, suggesting conclusions, and supporting decision making. _____ has multiple facets and approaches, encompassing diverse techniques under a variety of names, in different business, science, and social science domains.

Data mining is a particular _____ technique that focuses on modeling and knowledge discovery for predictive rather than purely descriptive purposes.

a. Power III
b. 180SearchAssistant
c. Data analysis
d. 6-3-5 Brainwriting

31. The _____ and the null hypothesis are the two rival hypotheses whose likelihoods are compared by a statistical hypothesis test. Usually the _____ is the possibility that an observed effect is genuine and the null hypothesis is the rival possibility that it has resulted from chance.

The classical (or frequentist) approach is to calculate the probability that the observed effect (or one more extreme) will occur if the null hypothesis is true.

a. Analysis of variance
b. Interval estimation
c. ACNielsen
d. Alternative hypothesis

32. In the absence of a more specific context, convergence denotes the approach toward a definite value, as time goes on; or to a definite point, a common view or opinion, or toward a fixed or equilibrium state. _____ is the adjectival form, and also a noun meaning an iterative approximation.

In mathematics, convergence describes limiting behaviour, particularly of an infinite sequence or series, toward some limit.

a. Strict liability
b. Good things come to those who wait
c. Convergent
d. Geo

33. _____ is the degree to which an operation is similar to (converges on) other operations that it theoretically should also be similar to. For instance, to show the _____ of a test of mathematics skills, the scores on the test can be correlated with scores on other tests that are also designed to measure basic mathematics ability. High correlations between the test scores would be evidence of a _____.

a. Criterion validity
b. Discriminant validity
c. Content validity
d. Convergent validity

34. In economics, _____ is the desire to own something and the ability to pay for it. The term _____ signifies the ability or the willingness to buy a particular commodity at a given point of time.

a. Market dominance
b. Market system
c. Discretionary spending
d. Demand

35. In research, and particularly psychology, _____ refers to an experimental artifact where participants form an interpretation of the experiment's purpose and unconsciously change their behavior accordingly. Pioneering research was conducted on _____ by Martin Orne. Typically, they are considered a confounding variable, exerting an effect on behavior other than that intended by the experimenter.

a. 6-3-5 Brainwriting
b. Power III
c. Demand characteristics
d. 180SearchAssistant

36. In algebra, the _____ of a polynomial with real or complex coefficients is a certain expression in the coefficients of the polynomial which is equal to zero if and only if the polynomial has a multiple root (i.e. a root with multiplicity greater than one) in the complex numbers. For example, the _____ of the quadratic polynomial

$$ax^2 + bx + c \text{ is } b^2 - 4ac.$$

The _____ of the cubic polynomial

$$ax^3 + bx^2 + cx + d \text{ is } b^2c^2 - 4ac^3 - 4b^3d - 27a^2d^2 + 18abcd.$$

a. Discriminant
b. Flighting
c. Lifestyle center
d. Consumption Map

37. _____ describes the degree to which the operationalization is not similar to (diverges from) other operationalizations that it theoretically should not be similar to.

Campbell and Fiske (1959) introduced the concept of _____ within their discussion on evaluating test validity. They stressed the importance of using both discriminant and convergent validation techniques when assessing new tests.

a. Predictive validity
b. Discriminant validity
c. Criterion validity
d. Convergent validity

38. _____ is the process by which a new idea or new product is accepted by the market. The rate of _____ is the speed that the new idea spreads from one consumer to the next. Adoption is similar to _____ except that it deals with the psychological processes an individual goes through, rather than an aggregate market process.

a. Kano model
b. Perceptual maps
c. Diffusion
d. Market development

Chapter 8. Observation Techniques, Experiments, and Test Markets

39. _____ is systematic determination of merit, worth, and significance of something or someone using criteria against a set of standards. _____ often is used to characterize and appraise subjects of interest in a wide range of human enterprises, including the arts, criminal justice, foundations and non-profit organizations, government, health care, and other human services.

Depending on the topic of interest, there are professional groups which look to the quality and rigor of the _____ process.

 a. Evaluation
 b. ACNielsen
 c. ADTECH
 d. AMAX

40. _____ are a vital part of the scientific method, since they can eliminate or minimise unintended influences such as researcher bias, environmental changes and biological variation. Controlled experiments are used to investigate the effect of a variable on a particular system. In a controlled one set of samples have been (or is believed to be) modified and the other set of samples are either expected to show no change (negative control) or expected to show a definite change (positive control.)
 a. Pearson's chi-square
 b. Clutter
 c. Scientific controls
 d. Little value placed on potential benefits

41. A _____ is a research instrument consisting of a series of questions and other prompts for the purpose of gathering information from respondents. Although they are often designed for statistical analysis of the responses, this is not always the case. The _____ was invented by Sir Francis Galton.
 a. Mystery shoppers
 b. Mystery shopping
 c. Market research
 d. Questionnaire

42. In statistics, an _____ is a term in a statistical model added when the effect of two or more variables is not simply additive. Such a term reflects that the effect of one variable depends on the values of one or more other variables.

Thus, for a response Y and two variables x_1 and x_2 an additive model would be:

$$Y = ax_1 + bx_2 + \text{error}$$

In contrast to this,

$$Y = ax_1 + bx_2 + c(x_1 \times x_2) + \text{error},$$

is an example of a model with an _____ between variables x_1 and x_2 ('error' refers to the random variable whose value by which y differs from the expected value of y.)

 a. ACNielsen
 b. Interaction
 c. AMAX
 d. ADTECH

43. The general definition of an _____ is an evaluation of a person, organization, system, process, project or product. _____s are performed to ascertain the validity and reliability of information; also to provide an assessment of a system's internal control. The goal of an _____ is to express an opinion on the person/organization/system (etc) in question, under evaluation based on work done on a test basis.
    a. ADTECH
    b. AMAX
    c. Audit
    d. ACNielsen

44. _____ is the imitation of some real thing, state of affairs, or process. The act of simulating something generally entails representing certain key characteristics or behaviors of a selected physical or abstract system.

    _____ is used in many contexts, including the modeling of natural systems or human systems in order to gain insight into their functioning.

    a. 180SearchAssistant
    b. Simulation
    c. 6-3-5 Brainwriting
    d. Power III

45. _____ is a broad label that refers to any individuals or households that use goods and services generated within the economy. The concept of a _____ is used in different contexts, so that the usage and significance of the term may vary.

    A _____ is a person who uses any product or service.

    a. Power III
    b. 180SearchAssistant
    c. 6-3-5 Brainwriting
    d. Consumer

46. In probability theory and statistics, _____ indicates the strength and direction of a linear relationship between two random variables. That is in contrast with the usage of the term in colloquial speech, denoting any relationship, not necessarily linear. In general statistical usage, _____ or co-relation refers to the departure of two random variables from independence.
    a. Mean
    b. Probability
    c. Frequency distribution
    d. Correlation

Chapter 9. Sampling: Theory and Design

1. The _____ of a statistical sample is the number of observations that constitute it. It is typically denoted n, a positive integer (natural number.)

Typically, all else being equal, a larger _____ leads to increased precision in estimates of various properties of the population.

   a. Data
   b. Heteroskedastic
   c. Frequency distribution
   d. Sample size

2. Sampling is the use of a subset of the population to represent the whole population. Probability sampling, or random sampling, is a sampling technique in which the probability of getting any particular sample may be calculated. _____ does not meet this criterion and should be used with caution.
   a. Quota sampling
   b. Power III
   c. Snowball sampling
   d. Nonprobability sampling

3. _____ is a way of expressing knowledge or belief that an event will occur or has occurred. In mathematics the concept has been given an exact meaning in _____ theory, that is used extensively in such areas of study as mathematics, statistics, finance, gambling, science, and philosophy to draw conclusions about the likelihood of potential events and the underlying mechanics of complex systems.
   a. Data
   b. Linear regression
   c. Heteroskedastic
   d. Probability

4. _____ is that part of statistical practice concerned with the selection of individual observations intended to yield some knowledge about a population of concern, especially for the purposes of statistical inference. Each observation measures one or more properties (weight, location, etc.) of an observable entity enumerated to distinguish objects or individuals.
   a. Sports Marketing Group
   b. AStore
   c. Richard Buckminster 'Bucky' Fuller
   d. Sampling

5. _____ is a term for unprocessed data, it is also known as primary data. It is a relative term _____ can be input to a computer program or used in manual analysis procedures such as gathering statistics from a survey.
   a. Shoppers Food ' Pharmacy
   b. Product manager
   c. Raw data
   d. Chief marketing officer

6. _____ refer to a collection of facts usually collected as the result of experience, observation or experiment or a set of premises. This may consist of numbers, words particularly as measurements or observations of a set of variables. _____ are often viewed as a lowest level of abstraction from which information and knowledge are derived.
   a. Sample size
   b. Mean
   c. Pearson product-moment correlation coefficient
   d. Data

7. A personal and cultural _____ is a relative ethic _____, an assumption upon which implementation can be extrapolated. A _____ system is a set of consistent _____s and measures that is soo not true. A principle _____ is a foundation upon which other _____s and measures of integrity are based.
   a. Perceptual maps
   b. Package-on-Package
   c. Supreme Court of the United States
   d. Value

8. In statistics, _____ or estimation error is the error caused by observing a sample instead of the whole population.

Chapter 9. Sampling: Theory and Design

An estimate of a quantity of interest, such as an average or percentage, will generally be subject to sample-to-sample variation. These variations in the possible sample values of a statistic can theoretically be expressed as _____s, although in practice the exact _____ is typically unknown.

a. Varimax rotation
c. Power III
b. Two-tailed test
d. Sampling error

9. In probability theory, the _____ states conditions under which the sum of a sufficiently large number of independent random variables, each with finite mean and variance, will be approximately normally distributed. More generally, a _____ is any of a set of weak-convergence results in probability theory. They all express the fact that a sum of many independent random variables will tend to be distributed according to one of a small set of 'attractor' (i.e. stable) distributions.

a. 180SearchAssistant
c. 6-3-5 Brainwriting
b. Power III
d. Central limit theorem

10. _____ is the examining of goods or services from retailers with the intent to purchase at that time. _____ is an activity of selection and/or purchase. In some contexts it is considered a leisure activity as well as an economic one.

a. Discount store
c. Hawkers
b. Shopping
d. Khodebshchik

11. In statistics, _____ is a collection of statistical models, and their associated procedures, in which the observed variance is partitioned into components due to different explanatory variables. The initial techniques of the _____ were developed by the statistician and geneticist R. A. Fisher in the 1920s and 1930s, and is sometimes known as Fisher's ANOVA or Fisher's _____, due to the use of Fisher's F-distribution as part of the test of statistical significance.

There are three conceptual classes of such models:

1. Fixed-effects models assumes that the data came from normal populations which may differ only in their means. (Model 1)
2. Random effects models assume that the data describe a hierarchy of different populations whose differences are constrained by the hierarchy. (Model 2)
3. Mixed-effect models describe situations where both fixed and random effects are present. (Model 3)

In practice, there are several types of ANOVA depending on the number of treatments and the way they are applied to the subjects in the experiment:

- One-way ANOVA is used to test for differences among two or more independent groups. Typically, however, the One-way ANOVA is used to test for differences among at least three groups, since the two-group case can be covered by a T-test (Gossett, 1908.)

a. ACNielsen
c. Analysis of variance
b. Interval estimation
d. Arithmetic mean

12. _____ is one of the four elements of marketing mix. An organization or set of organizations (go-betweens) involved in the process of making a product or service available for use or consumption by a consumer or business user.

The other three parts of the marketing mix are product, pricing, and promotion.

   a. Comparison-Shopping agent
   b. Japan Advertising Photographers' Association
   c. Better Living Through Chemistry
   d. Distribution

13. In probability theory and statistics, the _____ of a random variable, probability distribution, or sample is a measure of statistical dispersion, averaging the squared distance of its possible values from the expected value (mean.) Whereas the mean is a way to describe the location of a distribution, the _____ is a way to capture its scale or degree of being spread out. The unit of _____ is the square of the unit of the original variable.

   a. Sample size
   b. Correlation
   c. Standard deviation
   d. Variance

14. _____ is a computer program used for statistical analysis.

_____ (originally, Statistical Package for the Social Sciences) was released in its first version in 1968 after being founded by Norman Nie and C. Hadlai Hull. Nie was then a political science postgraduate at Stanford University, and now Research Professor in the Department of Political Science at Stanford and Professor Emeritus of Political Science at the University of Chicago.

   a. SPSS
   b. Power III
   c. 180SearchAssistant
   d. 6-3-5 Brainwriting

15. _____ a research method involving the use of questionnaires and/or statistical surveys to gather data about people and their thoughts and behaviours.

   a. Z-test
   b. Survey research
   c. T-test
   d. Control chart

16. _____s are biases in measurement which lead to the situation where the mean of many separate measurements differs significantly from the actual value of the measured attribute. All measurements are prone to _____s, often of several different types. Sources of _____ may be imperfect calibration of measurement instruments, changes in the environment which interfere with the measurement process and sometimes imperfect methods of observation can be either zero error or percentage error.

   a. Power III
   b. Systematic error
   c. 180SearchAssistant
   d. Systematic bias

17. In statistics, a _____ is an interval estimate of a population parameter. Instead of estimating the parameter by a single value, an interval likely to include the parameter is given. Thus, _____s are used to indicate the reliability of an estimate.

   a. Linear regression
   b. Sample mean
   c. T-test
   d. Confidence interval

Chapter 9. Sampling: Theory and Design

18. _____ is a process of gathering, modeling, and transforming data with the goal of highlighting useful information, suggesting conclusions, and supporting decision making. _____ has multiple facets and approaches, encompassing diverse techniques under a variety of names, in different business, science, and social science domains.

Data mining is a particular _____ technique that focuses on modeling and knowledge discovery for predictive rather than purely descriptive purposes.

a. Power III
c. 180SearchAssistant
b. 6-3-5 Brainwriting
d. Data analysis

19. In statistics, _____ is a simple measure of the variability or dispersion of a data set. A low _____ indicates that the data points tend to be very close to the same value (the mean), while high _____ indicates that the data are 'spread out' over a large range of values.

For example, the average height for adult men in the United States is about 70 inches, with a _____ of around 3 inches.

a. Statistically significant
c. Z-test
b. Pearson product-moment correlation coefficient
d. Standard deviation

20. In mathematics, an _____, or central tendency of a data set refers to a measure of the 'middle' or 'expected' value of the data set. There are many different descriptive statistics that can be chosen as a measurement of the central tendency of the data items.

An _____ is a single value that is meant to typify a list of values.

a. AMAX
c. ACNielsen
b. ADTECH
d. Average

21. In statistics, _____ has two related meanings:

- the arithmetic _____
- the expected value of a random variable, which is also called the population _____.

It is sometimes stated that the '_____' _____s average. This is incorrect if '_____' is taken in the specific sense of 'arithmetic _____' as there are different types of averages: the _____, median, and mode. For instance, average house prices almost always use the median value for the average. These three types of averages are all measures of locations.

a. Standard normal distribution
c. Mean
b. Heteroskedastic
d. Confidence interval

22. In mathematics and statistics, the arithmetic mean (or simply the mean) of a list of numbers is the sum of all of the list divided by the number of items in the list. If the list is a statistical population, then the mean of that population is called a population mean. If the list is a statistical sample, we call the resulting statistic a _____.

a. Null hypothesis
b. Coefficient of variation
c. Z-test
d. Sample mean

23. In statistics, a _____ is a dimensionless quantity derived by subtracting the population mean from an individual raw score and then dividing the difference by the population standard deviation. This conversion process is called standardizing or normalizing; however, 'normalizing' can refer to many types of ratios; see normalization (statistics) for more.

Yhey are also called z-values, z-scores, normal scores, and standardized variables; the use of 'Z' is because the normal distribution is also known as the 'Z distribution'.

a. Statistical hypothesis test
b. Sample size
c. Randomization
d. Standard score

24. _____ is defined by the American _____ Association as the activity, set of institutions, and processes for creating, communicating, delivering, and exchanging offerings that have value for customers, clients, partners, and society at large. The term developed from the original meaning which referred literally to going to market, as in shopping, or going to a market to sell goods or services.

_____ practice tends to be seen as a creative industry, which includes advertising, distribution and selling.

a. Product naming
b. Marketing myopia
c. Customer acquisition management
d. Marketing

25. Consumer market research is a form of applied sociology that concentrates on understanding the behaviours, whims and preferences, of consumers in a market-based economy, and aims to understand the effects and comparative success of marketing campaigns. The field of consumer _____ as a statistical science was pioneered by Arthur Nielsen with the founding of the ACNielsen Company in 1923 .

Thus _____ is the systematic and objective identification, collection, analysis, and dissemination of information for the purpose of assisting management in decision making related to the identification and solution of problems and opportunities in marketing.

a. Marketing Research
b. Marketing research process
c. Logit analysis
d. Focus group

26. _____ is a sampling technique used when 'natural' groupings are evident in a statistical population. It is often used in marketing research. In this technique, the total population is divided into these groups (or clusters) and a sample of the groups is selected.

a. Power III
b. Cluster sampling
c. Snowball sampling
d. Quota sampling

27. In economics, business, retail, and accounting, a _____ is the value of money that has been used up to produce something, and hence is not available for use anymore. In economics, a _____ is an alternative that is given up as a result of a decision. In business, the _____ may be one of acquisition, in which case the amount of money expended to acquire it is counted as _____.

a. Fixed costs	b. Transaction cost
c. Cost	d. Variable cost

28. Human beings are also considered to be _____ because they have the ability to change raw materials into valuable _____. The term Human _____ can also be defined as the skills, energies, talents, abilities and knowledge that are used for the production of goods or the rendering of services. While taking into account human beings as _____, the following things have to be kept in mind:

- The size of the population
- The capabilities of the individuals in that population

Many _____ cannot be consumed in their original form. They have to be processed in order to change them into more usable commodities.

a. 6-3-5 Brainwriting	b. Power III
c. Resources	d. 180SearchAssistant

29. _____ is anything that is intended to save time, energy or frustration. A _____ store at a petrol station, for example, sells items that have nothing to do with gasoline/petrol, but it saves the consumer from having to go to a grocery store. '_____' is a very relative term and its meaning tends to change over time.

a. MaxDiff	b. Marketing buzz
c. Demographic profile	d. Convenience

30. _____ is a type of nonprobability sampling which involves the sample being drawn from that part of the population which is close to hand. That is, a sample population selected because it is readily available and convenient. The researcher using such a sample cannot scientifically make generalizations about the total population from this sample because it would not be representative enough.

a. AMAX	b. Accidental sampling
c. ACNielsen	d. ADTECH

31. _____ is a form of communication that typically attempts to persuade potential customers to purchase or to consume more of a particular brand of product or service. 'While now central to the contemporary global economy and the reproduction of global production networks, it is only quite recently that _____ has been more than a marginal influence on patterns of sales and production. The formation of modern _____ was intimately bound up with the emergence of new forms of monopoly capitalism around the end of the 19th and beginning of the 20th century as one element in corporate strategies to create, organize and where possible control markets, especially for mass produced consumer goods.

a. ADTECH	b. AMAX
c. Advertising	d. ACNielsen

32. _____ is a specialized form of marketing research conducted to improve the efficiency of advertising. According to MarketConscious.com, 'It may focus on a specific ad or campaign, or may be directed at a more general understanding of how advertising works or how consumers use the information in advertising. It can entail a variety of research approaches, including psychological, sociological, economic, and other perspectives.'

1879 - N.W. Ayer conducts custom research in an attempt to win the advertising business of Nichols-Shepard Co., a manufacturer of agricultural machinery.

a. American Medical Association
c. Electrolux
b. INVISTA
d. Advertising Research

33. The _____ is a nonprofit industry association for creating, aggregating, synthesizing and sharing the knowledge in the fields of advertising and media. It was founded in 1936 by the Association of National Advertisers and the American Association of Advertising Agencies. Its stated mission is to improve the practice of advertising, marketing and media research in pursuit of more effective marketing and advertising communications.
   a. Advertising Research Foundation
   c. ACNielsen
   b. Intent scale translation
   d. IDDEA

34. Competitiveness is a comparative concept of the ability and performance of a firm, sub-sector or country to sell and supply goods and/or services in a given market. Although widely used in economics and business management, the usefulness of the concept, particularly in the context of national competitiveness, is vigorously disputed by economists, such as Paul Krugman .

The term may also be applied to markets, where it is used to refer to the extent to which the market structure may be regarded as perfectly _____.

   a. Geographical pricing
   c. Free trade zone
   b. Customs union
   d. Competitive

35. A _____ is the space, actual or metaphorical, in which a market operates. The term is also used in a trademark law context to denote the actual consumer environment, ie. the 'real world' in which products and services are provided and consumed.
   a. 180SearchAssistant
   c. Power III
   b. 6-3-5 Brainwriting
   d. Marketplace

36. _____ is either an activity of a living being (such as a human), consisting of receiving knowledge of the outside world through the senses, or the recording of data using scientific instruments. The term may also refer to any datum collected during this activity.

The scientific method requires _____s of nature to formulate and test hypotheses.

   a. ADTECH
   c. AMAX
   b. ACNielsen
   d. Observation

37. _____ in survey research refers to the ratio of number of people who answered the survey divided by the number of people in the sample. It is usually expressed in the form of a percentage.

Example: if 1,000 surveys were sent by mail, and 257 were successfully completed and returned, then the _____ would be 25.7 %.

   a. Sentence completion tests
   c. Power III
   b. Reference value
   d. Response rate

Chapter 9. Sampling: Theory and Design

38. The _____ is the number of new cases per unit of person-time at risk. In the same example as above, the _____ is 14 cases per 1000 person-years, because the incidence proportion (28 per 1,000) is divided by the number of years (two.) Using person-time rather than just time handles situations where the amount of observation time differs between people, or when the population at risk varies with time.
   a. ACNielsen
   b. ADTECH
   c. AMAX
   d. Incidence rate

39. In statistics, the _____ is a common measure of the correlation (linear dependence) between two variables X and Y. It is very widely used in the sciences as a measure of the strength of linear dependence between two variables, giving a value somewhere between +1 and -1 inclusive. It was first introduced by Francis Galton in the 1880s, and named after Karl Pearson.

In accordance with the usual convention, when calculated for an entire population, the Pearson product-moment correlation is typically designated by the analogous Greek letter, which in this case is ρ .

   a. Median
   b. Standard deviation
   c. Control chart
   d. Pearson product-moment correlation coefficient

40. In probability theory and statistics, _____ indicates the strength and direction of a linear relationship between two random variables. That is in contrast with the usage of the term in colloquial speech, denoting any relationship, not necessarily linear. In general statistical usage, _____ or co-relation refers to the departure of two random variables from independence.
   a. Mean
   b. Correlation
   c. Probability
   d. Frequency distribution

Chapter 10. Sampling: Methods and Planning

1. Sampling is the use of a subset of the population to represent the whole population. Probability sampling, or random sampling, is a sampling technique in which the probability of getting any particular sample may be calculated. _____ does not meet this criterion and should be used with caution.
   - a. Quota sampling
   - b. Nonprobability sampling
   - c. Snowball sampling
   - d. Power III

2. _____ is a way of expressing knowledge or belief that an event will occur or has occurred. In mathematics the concept has been given an exact meaning in _____ theory, that is used extensively in such areas of study as mathematics, statistics, finance, gambling, science, and philosophy to draw conclusions about the likelihood of potential events and the underlying mechanics of complex systems.
   - a. Data
   - b. Linear regression
   - c. Heteroskedastic
   - d. Probability

3. _____ is a sampling technique used when 'natural' groupings are evident in a statistical population. It is often used in marketing research. In this technique, the total population is divided into these groups (or clusters) and a sample of the groups is selected.
   - a. Cluster sampling
   - b. Power III
   - c. Snowball sampling
   - d. Quota sampling

4. _____ is anything that is intended to save time, energy or frustration. A _____ store at a petrol station, for example, sells items that have nothing to do with gasoline/petrol, but it saves the consumer from having to go to a grocery store. '_____' is a very relative term and its meaning tends to change over time.
   - a. Marketing buzz
   - b. MaxDiff
   - c. Demographic profile
   - d. Convenience

5. _____ is a type of nonprobability sampling which involves the sample being drawn from that part of the population which is close to hand. That is, a sample population selected because it is readily available and convenient. The researcher using such a sample cannot scientifically make generalizations about the total population from this sample because it would not be representative enough.
   - a. ADTECH
   - b. ACNielsen
   - c. AMAX
   - d. Accidental sampling

6. A _____ is a form of qualitative research in which a group of people are asked about their attitude towards a product, service, concept, advertisement, idea, or packaging. Questions are asked in an interactive group setting where participants are free to talk with other group members.

   Ernest Dichter originated the idea of having a 'group therapy' for products and this process is what became known as a _____.

   - a. Marketing research process
   - b. Cross tabulation
   - c. Logit analysis
   - d. Focus group

7. _____ is that part of statistical practice concerned with the selection of individual observations intended to yield some knowledge about a population of concern, especially for the purposes of statistical inference. Each observation measures one or more properties (weight, location, etc.) of an observable entity enumerated to distinguish objects or individuals.

a. Richard Buckminster 'Bucky' Fuller　　　b. Sports Marketing Group
c. AStore　　　d. Sampling

8. In statistics, _____ or estimation error is the error caused by observing a sample instead of the whole population.

An estimate of a quantity of interest, such as an average or percentage, will generally be subject to sample-to-sample variation. These variations in the possible sample values of a statistic can theoretically be expressed as _____s, although in practice the exact _____ is typically unknown.

a. Two-tailed test　　　b. Power III
c. Varimax rotation　　　d. Sampling error

9. In social science research, _____ is a technique for developing a research sample where existing study subjects recruit future subjects from among their acquaintances. Thus the sample group appears to grow like a rolling snowball. As the sample builds up, enough data is gathered to be useful for research.
a. Snowball sampling　　　b. Quota sampling
c. Power III　　　d. Nonprobability sampling

10. _____ a research method involving the use of questionnaires and/or statistical surveys to gather data about people and their thoughts and behaviours.
a. Control chart　　　b. Z-test
c. T-test　　　d. Survey research

11. In statistics, a _____ is an interval estimate of a population parameter. Instead of estimating the parameter by a single value, an interval likely to include the parameter is given. Thus, _____s are used to indicate the reliability of an estimate.
a. Sample mean　　　b. T-test
c. Linear regression　　　d. Confidence interval

12. A personal and cultural _____ is a relative ethic _____, an assumption upon which implementation can be extrapolated. A _____ system is a set of consistent _____s and measures that is soo not true. A principle _____ is a foundation upon which other _____s and measures of integrity are based.
a. Supreme Court of the United States　　　b. Value
c. Perceptual maps　　　d. Package-on-Package

13. In statistics, a simple random sample is a subset of individuals (a sample) chosen from a larger set (a population.) Each individual is chosen randomly and entirely by chance, such that each individual has the same probability of being chosen at any stage during the sampling process, and each subset of k individuals has the same probability of being chosen for the sample as any other subset of k individuals (.) This process and technique is known as _____, and should not be confused with Random Sampling.
a. Market analysis　　　b. Logit analysis
c. Focus group　　　d. Simple random sampling

14. In economics, business, retail, and accounting, a _____ is the value of money that has been used up to produce something, and hence is not available for use anymore. In economics, a _____ is an alternative that is given up as a result of a decision. In business, the _____ may be one of acquisition, in which case the amount of money expended to acquire it is counted as _____.
   a. Fixed costs
   b. Transaction cost
   c. Variable cost
   d. Cost

15. In statistics, _____ is a method of sampling from a population.

When sub-populations vary considerably, it is advantageous to sample each subpopulation (stratum) independently. Stratification is the process of grouping members of the population into relatively homogeneous subgroups before sampling.

   a. Coefficient of variation
   b. T-test
   c. Data
   d. Stratified sampling

16. The _____ is a professional association for marketers. As of 2008 it had approximately 40,000 members. There are collegiate chapters on 250 campuses.
   a. ACNielsen
   b. ADTECH
   c. AMAX
   d. American Marketing Association

17. The United States _____ is the government agency that is responsible for the United States Census. It also gathers other national demographic and economic data.
   a. Power III
   b. 180SearchAssistant
   c. 6-3-5 Brainwriting
   d. Census Bureau

18. A _____ is a retail establishment which specializes in selling a wide range of products without a single predominant merchandise line. _____s usually sell products including apparel, furniture, appliances, electronics, and additionally select other lines of products such as paint, hardware, toiletries, cosmetics, photographic equipment, jewelry, toys, and sporting goods. Certain _____s are further classified as discount _____s.
   a. Power III
   b. 180SearchAssistant
   c. 6-3-5 Brainwriting
   d. Department Store

19. _____ is a branch of philosophy which seeks to address questions about morality, such as how a moral outcome can be achieved in a specific situation (applied _____), how moral values should be determined (normative _____), what moral values people actually abide by (descriptive _____), what the fundamental semantic, ontological, and epistemic nature of _____ or morality is (meta-_____), and how moral capacity or moral agency develops and what its nature is (moral psychology.)

Socrates was one of the first Greek philosophers to encourage both scholars and the common citizen to turn their attention from the outside world to the condition of man. In this view, Knowledge having a bearing on human life was placed highest, all other knowledge being secondary.

   a. AMAX
   b. ACNielsen
   c. Ethics
   d. ADTECH

Chapter 10. Sampling: Methods and Planning

20. _____ is defined by the American _____ Association as the activity, set of institutions, and processes for creating, communicating, delivering, and exchanging offerings that have value for customers, clients, partners, and society at large. The term developed from the original meaning which referred literally to going to market, as in shopping, or going to a market to sell goods or services.

_____ practice tends to be seen as a creative industry, which includes advertising, distribution and selling.

   a. Product naming
   c. Customer acquisition management
   b. Marketing myopia
   d. Marketing

21. In the United States, the Office of Management and Budget (OMB) has produced a formal definition of metropolitan areas. These are referred to as '_____s' (_____s) and 'Combined Statistical Areas.' An earlier version of the _____ was the 'Standard _____' (SMetropolitan statistical area.) _____s are composed of counties and for some county equivalents.
   a. Power III
   c. Race and ethnicity in the United States Census
   b. Metropolitan statistical area
   d. 180SearchAssistant

22. _____ is the ability of an individual or group to seclude themselves or information about themselves and thereby reveal themselves selectively. The boundaries and content of what is considered private differ among cultures and individuals, but share basic common themes. _____ is sometimes related to anonymity, the wish to remain unnoticed or unidentified in the public realm.
   a. 180SearchAssistant
   c. Power III
   b. 6-3-5 Brainwriting
   d. Privacy

23. In _____, the population is first segmented into mutually exclusive sub-groups, just as in stratified sampling. Then judgment is used to select the subjects or units from each segment based on a specified proportion. For example, an interviewer may be told to sample 200 females and 300 males between the age of 45 and 60.
   a. Nonprobability sampling
   c. Power III
   b. Snowball sampling
   d. Quota sampling

24. A _____ is a structured collection of records or data that is stored in a computer system. The structure is achieved by organizing the data according to a _____ model. The model in most common use today is the relational model.
   a. Power III
   c. 180SearchAssistant
   b. 6-3-5 Brainwriting
   d. Database

25. A number of different _____s are indicated below.

- Randomized controlled trial
    - Double-blind randomized trial
    - Single-blind randomized trial
    - Non-blind trial
- Nonrandomized trial (quasi-experiment)
    - Interrupted time series design (measures on a sample or a series of samples from the same population are obtained several times before and after a manipulated event or a naturally occurring event) - considered a type of quasi-experiment

- Cohort study
    - Prospective cohort
    - Retrospective cohort
    - Time series study
- Case-control study
    - Nested case-control study
- Cross-sectional study
    - Community survey (a type of cross-sectional study)

When choosing a _____, many factors must be taken into account. Different types of studies are subject to different types of bias. For example, recall bias is likely to occur in cross-sectional or case-control studies where subjects are asked to recall exposure to risk factors.

a. Longitudinal studies
c. Study design
b. Power III
d. 180SearchAssistant

26. _____ is a computer program used for statistical analysis.

_____ (originally, Statistical Package for the Social Sciences) was released in its first version in 1968 after being founded by Norman Nie and C. Hadlai Hull. Nie was then a political science postgraduate at Stanford University, and now Research Professor in the Department of Political Science at Stanford and Professor Emeritus of Political Science at the University of Chicago.

a. 6-3-5 Brainwriting
c. Power III
b. SPSS
d. 180SearchAssistant

27. A _____, in the field of business and marketing, is a geographic region or demographic group used to gauge the viability of a product or service in the mass market prior to a wide scale roll-out. The criteria used to judge the acceptability of a _____ region or group include:

1. a population that is demographically similar to the proposed target market; and
2. relative isolation from densely populated media markets so that advertising to the test audience can be efficient and economical.

Chapter 10. Sampling: Methods and Planning

The _____ ideally aims to duplicate 'everything' - promotion and distribution as well as `product' - on a smaller scale. The technique replicates, typically in one area, what is planned to occur in a national launch; and the results are very carefully monitored, so that they can be extrapolated to projected national results. The `area' may be any one of the following:

- Television area
- Test town
- Residential neighborhood
- Test site

A number of decisions have to be taken about any _____:

- Which _____?
- What is to be tested?
- How long a test?
- What are the success criteria?

The simple go or no-go decision, together with the related reduction of risk, is normally the main justification for the expense of _____s. At the same time, however, such _____s can be used to test specific elements of a new product's marketing mix; possibly the version of the product itself, the promotional message and media spend, the distribution channels and the price.

a. 180SearchAssistant
b. Preadolescence
c. Power III
d. Test market

28. _____ refer to a collection of facts usually collected as the result of experience, observation or experiment or a set of premises. This may consist of numbers, words particularly as measurements or observations of a set of variables. _____ are often viewed as a lowest level of abstraction from which information and knowledge are derived.

a. Mean
b. Data
c. Sample size
d. Pearson product-moment correlation coefficient

29. _____ is a process of gathering, modeling, and transforming data with the goal of highlighting useful information, suggesting conclusions, and supporting decision making. _____ has multiple facets and approaches, encompassing diverse techniques under a variety of names, in different business, science, and social science domains.

Data mining is a particular _____ technique that focuses on modeling and knowledge discovery for predictive rather than purely descriptive purposes.

a. Power III
b. 180SearchAssistant
c. 6-3-5 Brainwriting
d. Data analysis

30. _____ is a type of research conducted because a problem has not been clearly defined. _____ helps determine the best research design, data collection method and selection of subjects. Given its fundamental nature, _____ often concludes that a perceived problem does not actually exist.

Chapter 10. Sampling: Methods and Planning

a. Intent scale translation
c. ACNielsen
b. IDDEA
d. Exploratory research

31. Human beings are also considered to be _____ because they have the ability to change raw materials into valuable _____. The term Human _____ can also be defined as the skills, energies, talents, abilities and knowledge that are used for the production of goods or the rendering of services. While taking into account human beings as _____, the following things have to be kept in mind:

- The size of the population
- The capabilities of the individuals in that population

Many _____ cannot be consumed in their original form. They have to be processed in order to change them into more usable commodities.

a. 6-3-5 Brainwriting
c. Power III
b. 180SearchAssistant
d. Resources

32. _____ is a term used to describe a process of preparing and collecting data - for example as part of a process improvement or similar project.

_____ usually takes place early on in an improvement project, and is often formalised through a _____ Plan which often contains the following activity.

1. Pre collection activity - Agree goals, target data, definitions, methods
2. Collection - _____
3. Present Findings - usually involves some form of sorting analysis and/or presentation.

A formal _____ process is necessary as it ensures that data gathered is both defined and accurate and that subsequent decisions based on arguments embodied in the findings are valid. The process provides both a baseline from which to measure from and in certain cases a target on what to improve. Types of _____ 1-By mail questionnaires 2-By personal interview

- Six sigma
- Sampling (statistics)

a. 180SearchAssistant
c. Data collection
b. 6-3-5 Brainwriting
d. Power III

33. The _____ of a statistical sample is the number of observations that constitute it. It is typically denoted n, a positive integer (natural number.)

Typically, all else being equal, a larger _____ leads to increased precision in estimates of various properties of the population.

a. Sample size
b. Data
c. Heteroskedastic
d. Frequency distribution

34. In statistics, the _____ is a common measure of the correlation (linear dependence) between two variables X and Y. It is very widely used in the sciences as a measure of the strength of linear dependence between two variables, giving a value somewhere between +1 and -1 inclusive. It was first introduced by Francis Galton in the 1880s, and named after Karl Pearson.

In accordance with the usual convention, when calculated for an entire population, the Pearson product-moment correlation is typically designated by the analogous Greek letter, which in this case is ρ.

a. Standard deviation
b. Control chart
c. Pearson product-moment correlation coefficient
d. Median

35. In probability theory and statistics, _____ indicates the strength and direction of a linear relationship between two random variables. That is in contrast with the usage of the term in colloquial speech, denoting any relationship, not necessarily linear. In general statistical usage, _____ or co-relation refers to the departure of two random variables from independence.

a. Probability
b. Correlation
c. Mean
d. Frequency distribution

Chapter 11. Overview of Measurement: Construct Development and Scale Measurement

1. A personal and cultural _____ is a relative ethic _____, an assumption upon which implementation can be extrapolated. A _____ system is a set of consistent _____s and measures that is soo not true. A principle _____ is a foundation upon which other _____s and measures of integrity are based.
   a. Package-on-Package
   b. Supreme Court of the United States
   c. Perceptual maps
   d. Value

2. In social science and psychometrics, _____ refers to whether a scale measures or correlates with a theorized psychological construct (such as 'fluid intelligence'.) It is related to the theoretical ideas behind the personality trait under consideration; a non-existent concept in the physical sense may be suggested as a method of organising how personality can be viewed. The unobservable idea of a unidimensional easier-to-harder dimension must be 'constructed' in the words of human language and graphics.
   a. Discriminant validity
   b. Construct validity
   c. Predictive validity
   d. Criterion validity

3. In psychometrics, _____ refers to the extent to which a measure represents all facets of a given social construct. For example, a depression scale may lack _____ if it only assesses the affective dimension of depression but fails to take into account the behavioral dimension. An element of subjectivity exists in relation to determining _____, which requires a degree of agreement about what a particular personality trait such as extraversion represents.
   a. Predictive validity
   b. Convergent validity
   c. Criterion validity
   d. Content validity

4. In the absence of a more specific context, convergence denotes the approach toward a definite value, as time goes on; or to a definite point, a common view or opinion, or toward a fixed or equilibrium state. _____ is the adjectival form, and also a noun meaning an iterative approximation.

   In mathematics, convergence describes limiting behaviour, particularly of an infinite sequence or series, toward some limit.
   a. Good things come to those who wait
   b. Geo
   c. Strict liability
   d. Convergent

5. _____ is the degree to which an operation is similar to (converges on) other operations that it theoretically should also be similar to. For instance, to show the _____ of a test of mathematics skills, the scores on the test can be correlated with scores on other tests that are also designed to measure basic mathematics ability. High correlations between the test scores would be evidence of a _____.
   a. Convergent validity
   b. Content validity
   c. Criterion validity
   d. Discriminant validity

6. In algebra, the _____ of a polynomial with real or complex coefficients is a certain expression in the coefficients of the polynomial which is equal to zero if and only if the polynomial has a multiple root (i.e. a root with multiplicity greater than one) in the complex numbers. For example, the _____ of the quadratic polynomial

$ax^2 + bx + c$ is $b^2 - 4ac$.

Chapter 11. Overview of Measurement: Construct Development and Scale Measurement 111

The _____ of the cubic polynomial

$$ax^3 + bx^2 + cx + d \text{ is } b^2c^2 - 4ac^3 - 4b^3d - 27a^2d^2 + 18abcd.$$

    a. Lifestyle center   b. Consumption Map
    c. Flighting   d. Discriminant

7. _____ describes the degree to which the operationalization is not similar to (diverges from) other operationalizations that it theoretically should not be similar to.

Campbell and Fiske (1959) introduced the concept of _____ within their discussion on evaluating test validity. They stressed the importance of using both discriminant and convergent validation techniques when assessing new tests.

    a. Predictive validity   b. Convergent validity
    c. Criterion validity   d. Discriminant validity

8. _____, a business term, is a measure of how products and services supplied by a company meet or surpass customer expectation. It is seen as a key performance indicator within business and is part of the four perspectives of a Balanced Scorecard.

In a competitive marketplace where businesses compete for customers, _____ is seen as a key differentiator and increasingly has become a key element of business strategy.

    a. Psychological pricing   b. Supplier diversity
    c. Customer base   d. Customer satisfaction

9. Cognition is the scientific term for 'the process of thought.' Its usage varies in different ways in accord with different disciplines: For example, in psychology and _____ science it refers to an information processing view of an individual's psychological functions. Other interpretations of the meaning of cognition link it to the development of concepts; individual minds, groups, organizations, and even larger coalitions of entities, can be modelled as 'societies' (Society of Mind), which cooperate to form concepts.

The autonomous elements of each 'society' would have the opportunity to demonstrate emergent behavior in the face of some crisis or opportunity.

    a. Power III   b. 6-3-5 Brainwriting
    c. 180SearchAssistant   d. Cognitive

10. _____ refer to a collection of facts usually collected as the result of experience, observation or experiment or a set of premises. This may consist of numbers, words particularly as measurements or observations of a set of variables. _____ are often viewed as a lowest level of abstraction from which information and knowledge are derived.

Chapter 11. Overview of Measurement: Construct Development and Scale Measurement

a. Pearson product-moment correlation coefficient
b. Sample size
c. Mean
d. Data

11. _____ is a term used to describe a process of preparing and collecting data - for example as part of a process improvement or similar project.

_____ usually takes place early on in an improvement project, and is often formalised through a _____ Plan which often contains the following activity.

1. Pre collection activity - Agree goals, target data, definitions, methods
2. Collection - _____
3. Present Findings - usually involves some form of sorting analysis and/or presentation.

A formal _____ process is necessary as it ensures that data gathered is both defined and accurate and that subsequent decisions based on arguments embodied in the findings are valid . The process provides both a baseline from which to measure from and in certain cases a target on what to improve. Types of _____ 1-By mail questionnaires 2-By personal interview

- Six sigma
- Sampling (statistics)

a. Data collection
b. 180SearchAssistant
c. 6-3-5 Brainwriting
d. Power III

12. A number of different _____s are indicated below.

- Randomized controlled trial
    - Double-blind randomized trial
    - Single-blind randomized trial
    - Non-blind trial
- Nonrandomized trial (quasi-experiment)
    - Interrupted time series design (measures on a sample or a series of samples from the same population are obtained several times before and after a manipulated event or a naturally occurring event) - considered a type of quasi-experiment

- Cohort study
    - Prospective cohort
    - Retrospective cohort
    - Time series study
- Case-control study
    - Nested case-control study
- Cross-sectional study
    - Community survey (a type of cross-sectional study)

Chapter 11. Overview of Measurement: Construct Development and Scale Measurement

When choosing a _____, many factors must be taken into account. Different types of studies are subject to different types of bias. For example, recall bias is likely to occur in cross-sectional or case-control studies where subjects are asked to recall exposure to risk factors.

a. 180SearchAssistant
b. Longitudinal studies
c. Power III
d. Study design

13. The '_____' is an expression which typically refers to the theory of scale types developed by the Harvard psychologist Stanley Smith Stevens In this article Stevens claimed that all measurement in science was conducted using four different types of numerical scales which he called 'nominal', 'ordinal', 'interval' and 'ratio'.

a. Levels of measurement
b. 6-3-5 Brainwriting
c. Power III
d. 180SearchAssistant

14. _____ is a statistical method used to examine how reliable a test is: A test is performed twice, e.g., the same test is given to a group of subjects at two different times. Each subject should score different than the other subjects, but if the test is reliable then each subject should score the same in both test.

Valentin Rousson, Theo Gasser, and Burkhardt Seifert, (2002) 'Assessing intrarater, interrater and _____ reliability of continuous measurements,' Statistics in Medicine 21:3431-3446.

a. Test-retest
b. 180SearchAssistant
c. Power III
d. 6-3-5 Brainwriting

15. In statistics and research, _____ is a measure based on the correlations between different items on the same test (or the same subscale on a larger test.) It measures whether several items that propose to measure the same general construct produce similar scores. For example, if a respondent expressed agreement with the statements 'I like to ride bicycles' and 'I've enjoyed riding bicycles in the past', and disagreement with the statement 'I hate bicycles', this would be indicative of good _____ of the test.

a. ACNielsen
b. ADTECH
c. AMAX
d. Internal consistency

16. In statistics, _____ has two related meanings:

- the arithmetic _____
- the expected value of a random variable, which is also called the population _____.

It is sometimes stated that the '_____' _____s average. This is incorrect if '_____' is taken in the specific sense of 'arithmetic _____' as there are different types of averages: the _____, median, and mode. For instance, average house prices almost always use the median value for the average. These three types of averages are all measures of locations.

a. Confidence interval
b. Heteroskedastic
c. Standard normal distribution
d. Mean

114 Chapter 11. Overview of Measurement: Construct Development and Scale Measurement

17. In probability theory and statistics, a _____ is described as the number separating the higher half of a sample, a population from the lower half. The _____ of a finite list of numbers can be found by arranging all the observations from lowest value to highest value and picking the middle one. If there is an even number of observations, the _____ is not unique, so one often takes the mean of the two middle values.

   a. Statistically significant
   b. Frequency distribution
   c. Linear regression
   d. Median

18. _____ is the process of making something random; this means:

   - Generating a random permutation of a sequence (such as when shuffling cards.)
   - Selecting a random sample of a population (important in statistical sampling.)
   - Generating random numbers: see Random number generation.
   - Transforming a data stream using a scrambler in telecommunications.

   _____ is used extensively in the field of gambling (or generally being random.) Imperfect _____ may allow a skilled gambler to have an advantage, so much research has been devoted to effective _____. A classic example of _____ is shuffling playing cards.

   _____ is a core principle in the statistical theory of design of experiments.

   a. Statistics
   b. Randomization
   c. Sample size
   d. Standard deviation

19. _____ is a computer program used for statistical analysis.

   _____ (originally, Statistical Package for the Social Sciences) was released in its first version in 1968 after being founded by Norman Nie and C. Hadlai Hull. Nie was then a political science postgraduate at Stanford University, and now Research Professor in the Department of Political Science at Stanford and Professor Emeritus of Political Science at the University of Chicago.

   a. 180SearchAssistant
   b. Power III
   c. 6-3-5 Brainwriting
   d. SPSS

20. In statistics, _____ is a simple measure of the variability or dispersion of a data set. A low _____ indicates that the data points tend to be very close to the same value (the mean), while high _____ indicates that the data are 'spread out' over a large range of values.

   For example, the average height for adult men in the United States is about 70 inches, with a _____ of around 3 inches.

   a. Pearson product-moment correlation coefficient
   b. Statistically significant
   c. Standard deviation
   d. Z-test

21. In mathematics, an _____, or central tendency of a data set refers to a measure of the 'middle' or 'expected' value of the data set. There are many different descriptive statistics that can be chosen as a measurement of the central tendency of the data items.

Chapter 11. Overview of Measurement: Construct Development and Scale Measurement 115

An _____ is a single value that is meant to typify a list of values.

a. AMAX
b. ADTECH
c. ACNielsen
d. Average

22. _____ is one of the four elements of marketing mix. An organization or set of organizations (go-betweens) involved in the process of making a product or service available for use or consumption by a consumer or business user.

The other three parts of the marketing mix are product, pricing, and promotion.

a. Japan Advertising Photographers' Association
b. Comparison-Shopping agent
c. Better Living Through Chemistry
d. Distribution

23. In statistics, a _____ is a tabulation of the values that one or more variables take in a sample.

Univariate _____s are often presented as lists, ordered by quantity, showing the number of times each value appears. For example, if 100 people rate a five-point Likert scale assessing their agreement with a statement on a scale on which 1 denotes strong agreement and 5 strong disagreement, the _____ of their responses might look like:

This simple tabulation has two drawbacks.

a. Statistics
b. Confidence interval
c. Survey research
d. Frequency distribution

24. In descriptive statistics, the _____ is the length of the smallest interval which contains all the data. It is calculated by subtracting the smallest observation (sample minimum) from the greatest (sample maximum) and provides an indication of statistical dispersion.

It is measured in the same units as the data.

a. Personalization
b. Japan Advertising Photographers' Association
c. Just-In-Case
d. Range

25. A _____ is a subgroup of people or organizations sharing one or more characteristics that cause them to have similar product and/or service needs. A true _____ meets all of the following criteria: it is distinct from other segments (different segments have different needs), it is homogeneous within the segment (exhibits common needs); it responds similarly to a market stimulus, and it can be reached by a market intervention. The term is also used when consumers with identical product and/or service needs are divided up into groups so they can be charged different amounts.

a. Production orientation
b. Commercial planning
c. Market segment
d. Customer insight

116 *Chapter 11. Overview of Measurement: Construct Development and Scale Measurement*

26. In probability theory and statistics, _____ indicates the strength and direction of a linear relationship between two random variables. That is in contrast with the usage of the term in colloquial speech, denoting any relationship, not necessarily linear. In general statistical usage, _____ or co-relation refers to the departure of two random variables from independence.
   a. Frequency distribution
   b. Mean
   c. Probability
   d. Correlation

27. Human beings are also considered to be _____ because they have the ability to change raw materials into valuable _____. The term Human _____ can also be defined as the skills, energies, talents, abilities and knowledge that are used for the production of goods or the rendering of services. While taking into account human beings as _____, the following things have to be kept in mind:

   • The size of the population
   • The capabilities of the individuals in that population

   Many _____ cannot be consumed in their original form. They have to be processed in order to change them into more usable commodities.

   a. 180SearchAssistant
   b. Power III
   c. 6-3-5 Brainwriting
   d. Resources

28. The loyalty business model is a business model used in strategic management in which company resources are employed so as to increase the loyalty of customers and other stakeholders in the expectation that corporate objectives will be met or surpassed. A typical example of this type of model is: quality of product or service leads to customer satisfaction, which leads to _____, which leads to profitability.

   Fredrick Reichheld (1996) expanded the loyalty business model beyond customers and employees.

   a. Power III
   b. Customer loyalty
   c. 180SearchAssistant
   d. 6-3-5 Brainwriting

29. _____ or _____ data refers to selected population characteristics as used in government, marketing or opinion research, or the _____ profiles used in such research. Note the distinction from the term 'demography' Commonly-used _____ include race, age, income, disabilities, mobility (in terms of travel time to work or number of vehicles available), educational attainment, home ownership, employment status, and even location.
   a. AStore
   b. African Americans
   c. Demographic
   d. Albert Einstein

30. In statistics, the _____ is a common measure of the correlation (linear dependence) between two variables X and Y. It is very widely used in the sciences as a measure of the strength of linear dependence between two variables, giving a value somewhere between +1 and -1 inclusive. It was first introduced by Francis Galton in the 1880s, and named after Karl Pearson.

In accordance with the usual convention, when calculated for an entire population, the Pearson product-moment correlation is typically designated by the analogous Greek letter, which in this case is ρ.

a. Standard deviation
b. Control chart
c. Median
d. Pearson product-moment correlation coefficient

Chapter 12. Attitude Scale Measurements Used in Marketing Research

1. A _____ is a psychometric scale commonly used in questionnaires, and is the most widely used scale in survey research. When responding to a Likert questionnaire item, respondents specify their level of agreement to a statement. The scale is named after its inventor, psychologist Rensis Likert.
   - a. Semantic differential
   - b. Power III
   - c. Factor analysis
   - d. Likert scale

2. A personal and cultural _____ is a relative ethic _____, an assumption upon which implementation can be extrapolated. A _____ system is a set of consistent _____s and measures that is soo not true. A principle _____ is a foundation upon which other _____s and measures of integrity are based.
   - a. Perceptual maps
   - b. Supreme Court of the United States
   - c. Package-on-Package
   - d. Value

3. In environmental modeling and especially in hydrology, a _____ model means a model that is acceptably consistent with observed natural processes, i.e. that simulates well, for example, observed river discharge. It is a key concept of the so-called Generalized Likelihood Uncertainty Estimation (GLUE) methodology to quantify how uncertain environmental predictions are.
   - a. Behavioral
   - b. 6-3-5 Brainwriting
   - c. 180SearchAssistant
   - d. Power III

4. Cognition is the scientific term for 'the process of thought.' Its usage varies in different ways in accord with different disciplines: For example, in psychology and _____ science it refers to an information processing view of an individual's psychological functions. Other interpretations of the meaning of cognition link it to the development of concepts; individual minds, groups, organizations, and even larger coalitions of entities, can be modelled as 'societies' (Society of Mind), which cooperate to form concepts.

   The autonomous elements of each 'society' would have the opportunity to demonstrate emergent behavior in the face of some crisis or opportunity.

   - a. Cognitive
   - b. 180SearchAssistant
   - c. 6-3-5 Brainwriting
   - d. Power III

5. _____ is a broad label that refers to any individuals or households that use goods and services generated within the economy. The concept of a _____ is used in different contexts, so that the usage and significance of the term may vary.

   A _____ is a person who uses any product or service.

   - a. Consumer
   - b. 6-3-5 Brainwriting
   - c. 180SearchAssistant
   - d. Power III

6. _____ is the study of when, why, how, where and what people do or do not buy products. It blends elements from psychology, sociology, social psychology, anthropology and economics. It attempts to understand the buyer decision making process, both individually and in groups. It studies characteristics of individual consumers such as demographics and behavioural variables in an attempt to understand people's wants. It also tries to assess influences on the consumer from groups such as family, friends, reference groups, and society in general.

a. Communal marketing
c. Consumer confidence
b. Multidimensional scaling
d. Consumer Behavior

7. _____ is a type of a rating scale designed to measure the connotative meaning of objects, events, and concepts. The connotations are used to derive the attitude towards the given object, event or concept.

Osgood's _____ was designed to measure the connotative meaning of concepts.

a. Semantic differential
c. Power III
b. Factor analysis
d. Likert scale

8. In statistics, _____ is a collection of statistical models, and their associated procedures, in which the observed variance is partitioned into components due to different explanatory variables. The initial techniques of the _____ were developed by the statistician and geneticist R. A. Fisher in the 1920s and 1930s, and is sometimes known as Fisher's ANOVA or Fisher's _____, due to the use of Fisher's F-distribution as part of the test of statistical significance.

There are three conceptual classes of such models:

1. Fixed-effects models assumes that the data came from normal populations which may differ only in their means. (Model 1)
2. Random effects models assume that the data describe a hierarchy of different populations whose differences are constrained by the hierarchy. (Model 2)
3. Mixed-effect models describe situations where both fixed and random effects are present. (Model 3)

In practice, there are several types of ANOVA depending on the number of treatments and the way they are applied to the subjects in the experiment:

- One-way ANOVA is used to test for differences among two or more independent groups. Typically, however, the One-way ANOVA is used to test for differences among at least three groups, since the two-group case can be covered by a T-test (Gossett, 1908.)

a. Arithmetic mean
c. Interval estimation
b. ACNielsen
d. Analysis of variance

9. In probability theory and statistics, the _____ of a random variable, probability distribution, or sample is a measure of statistical dispersion, averaging the squared distance of its possible values from the expected value (mean.) Whereas the mean is a way to describe the location of a distribution, the _____ is a way to capture its scale or degree of being spread out. The unit of _____ is the square of the unit of the original variable.

a. Correlation
c. Variance
b. Sample size
d. Standard deviation

10. _____ is an American firm that measures media audiences, including television, radio, theatre films (via the AMC MAP program) and newspapers. _____, headquartered in New York City and operating primarily from Chicago, is best-known for the Nielsen Ratings, a measurement of television viewership.

Chapter 12. Attitude Scale Measurements Used in Marketing Research

_____, the preeminent media research company in the world, began as a division of ACNielsen, a marketing research firm.

a. Nielsen Media Research
b. Hennes ' Mauritz
c. CoolBrands
d. Green Earth Market

11. _____ is a type of cognitive bias which can affect the results of a statistical survey if respondents answer questions in the way they think the questioner wants them to answer rather than according to their true beliefs. This may occur if the questioner is obviously angling for a particular answer (as in push polling) or if the respondent wishes to please the questioner by answering what appears to be the 'morally right' answer. An example of the latter might be if a woman surveys a man on his attitudes to domestic violence, or someone who obviously cares about the environment asks people how much they value a wilderness area.

a. 180SearchAssistant
b. Power III
c. Von Restorff effect
d. Response bias

12. _____ is a standard point of view or personal prejudice. especially when the tendency interferes with the ability to be impartial, unprejudiced, or objective. The term _____ed is used to describe an action, judgment, or other outcome influenced by a prejudged perspective.

a. 180SearchAssistant
b. 6-3-5 Brainwriting
c. Bias
d. Power III

13. _____ is the process of making something random; this means:

- Generating a random permutation of a sequence (such as when shuffling cards.)
- Selecting a random sample of a population (important in statistical sampling.)
- Generating random numbers: see Random number generation.
- Transforming a data stream using a scrambler in telecommunications.

_____ is used extensively in the field of gambling (or generally being random.) Imperfect _____ may allow a skilled gambler to have an advantage, so much research has been devoted to effective _____. A classic example of _____ is shuffling playing cards.

_____ is a core principle in the statistical theory of design of experiments.

a. Sample size
b. Randomization
c. Statistics
d. Standard deviation

14. In the mathematical discipline of graph theory a _____ or edge-independent set in a graph is a set of edges without common vertices. It may also be an entire graph consisting of edges without common vertices.

Given a graph G = (V,E), a _____ M in G is a set of pairwise non-adjacent edges; that is, no two edges share a common vertex.

Chapter 12. Attitude Scale Measurements Used in Marketing Research

a. 180SearchAssistant
b. Matching
c. 6-3-5 Brainwriting
d. Power III

15. A _____ is a retail establishment which specializes in selling a wide range of products without a single predominant merchandise line. _____s usually sell products including apparel, furniture, appliances, electronics, and additionally select other lines of products such as paint, hardware, toiletries, cosmetics, photographic equipment, jewelery, toys, and sporting goods. Certain _____s are further classified as discount _____s.

a. 180SearchAssistant
b. Department Store
c. Power III
d. 6-3-5 Brainwriting

16. A _____ is a statement or claim that a particular event will occur in the future in more certain terms than a forecast. The etymology of this word is Latin . In regards to predicting the future Howard H. Stevenson Says, ' _____ is at least two things: Important and hard.' Important, because we have to act, and hard because we have to realize the future we want, and what is the best way to get there.

a. Power III
b. Prediction
c. 6-3-5 Brainwriting
d. 180SearchAssistant

17. In grammar, the _____ is the form of an adjective or adverb which denotes the degree or grade by which a person, thing and is used in this context with a subordinating conjunction, such as than, as...as, etc.

The structure of a _____ in English consists normally of the positive form of the adjective or adverb, plus the suffix -er e.g. 'he is taller than his father is', or 'the village is less picturesque than the town nearby'.

a. 6-3-5 Brainwriting
b. Comparative
c. 180SearchAssistant
d. Power III

18. _____, a business term, is a measure of how products and services supplied by a company meet or surpass customer expectation. It is seen as a key performance indicator within business and is part of the four perspectives of a Balanced Scorecard.

In a competitive marketplace where businesses compete for customers, _____ is seen as a key differentiator and increasingly has become a key element of business strategy.

a. Customer satisfaction
b. Customer base
c. Psychological pricing
d. Supplier diversity

19. _____ are used to collect quantitative information about items in a population. Surveys of human populations and institutions are common in political polling and government, health, social science and marketing research. A survey may focus on opinions or factual information depending on its purpose, and many surveys involve administering questions to individuals.

a. BeyondROI
b. Convergent
c. Gross Margin Return on Inventory Investment
d. Statistical surveys

Chapter 12. Attitude Scale Measurements Used in Marketing Research

20. _____ is defined by the American _____ Association as the activity, set of institutions, and processes for creating, communicating, delivering, and exchanging offerings that have value for customers, clients, partners, and society at large. The term developed from the original meaning which referred literally to going to market, as in shopping, or going to a market to sell goods or services.

_____ practice tends to be seen as a creative industry, which includes advertising, distribution and selling.

a. Product naming
c. Customer acquisition management
b. Marketing
d. Marketing myopia

21. Consumer market research is a form of applied sociology that concentrates on understanding the behaviours, whims and preferences, of consumers in a market-based economy, and aims to understand the effects and comparative success of marketing campaigns. The field of consumer _____ as a statistical science was pioneered by Arthur Nielsen with the founding of the ACNielsen Company in 1923.

Thus _____ is the systematic and objective identification, collection, analysis, and dissemination of information for the purpose of assisting management in decision making related to the identification and solution of problems and opportunities in marketing.

a. Focus group
c. Marketing research process
b. Logit analysis
d. Marketing Research

22. Human beings are also considered to be _____ because they have the ability to change raw materials into valuable _____. The term Human _____ can also be defined as the skills, energies, talents, abilities and knowledge that are used for the production of goods or the rendering of services. While taking into account human beings as _____, the following things have to be kept in mind:

- The size of the population
- The capabilities of the individuals in that population

Many _____ cannot be consumed in their original form. They have to be processed in order to change them into more usable commodities.

a. 6-3-5 Brainwriting
c. Power III
b. 180SearchAssistant
d. Resources

23. In algebra, the _____ of a polynomial with real or complex coefficients is a certain expression in the coefficients of the polynomial which is equal to zero if and only if the polynomial has a multiple root (i.e. a root with multiplicity greater than one) in the complex numbers. For example, the _____ of the quadratic polynomial

$ax^2 + bx + c$ is $b^2 - 4ac$.

The _____ of the cubic polynomial

$ax^3 + bx^2 + cx + d$ is $b^2c^2 - 4ac^3 - 4b^3d - 27a^2d^2 + 18abcd$.

Chapter 12. Attitude Scale Measurements Used in Marketing Research

a. Discriminant
c. Lifestyle center
b. Consumption Map
d. Flighting

24. Linear _____ and the related Fisher's linear discriminant are methods used in statistics and machine learning to find the linear combination of features which best separate two or more classes of objects or events. The resulting combination may be used as a linear classifier, or, more commonly, for dimensionality reduction before later classification.

LDiscriminant analysis is closely related to ANOVA (analysis of variance) and regression analysis, which also attempt to express one dependent variable as a linear combination of other features or measurements.

a. Multiple discriminant analysis
c. Linear discriminant analysis
b. Geodemographic segmentation
d. Discriminant analysis

25. The _____ is a professional association for marketers. As of 2008 it had approximately 40,000 members. There are collegiate chapters on 250 campuses.
a. ACNielsen
c. ADTECH
b. AMAX
d. American Marketing Association

26. _____ is a branch of philosophy which seeks to address questions about morality, such as how a moral outcome can be achieved in a specific situation (applied _____), how moral values should be determined (normative _____), what moral values people actually abide by (descriptive _____), what the fundamental semantic, ontological, and epistemic nature of _____ or morality is (meta-_____), and how moral capacity or moral agency develops and what its nature is (moral psychology.)

Socrates was one of the first Greek philosophers to encourage both scholars and the common citizen to turn their attention from the outside world to the condition of man. In this view, Knowledge having a bearing on human life was placed highest, all other knowledge being secondary.

a. ACNielsen
c. ADTECH
b. AMAX
d. Ethics

27. _____ is the ability of an individual or group to seclude themselves or information about themselves and thereby reveal themselves selectively. The boundaries and content of what is considered private differ among cultures and individuals, but share basic common themes. _____ is sometimes related to anonymity, the wish to remain unnoticed or unidentified in the public realm.
a. 6-3-5 Brainwriting
c. Power III
b. Privacy
d. 180SearchAssistant

28. The loyalty business model is a business model used in strategic management in which company resources are employed so as to increase the loyalty of customers and other stakeholders in the expectation that corporate objectives will be met or surpassed. A typical example of this type of model is: quality of product or service leads to customer satisfaction, which leads to _____, which leads to profitability.

Fredrick Reichheld (1996) expanded the loyalty business model beyond customers and employees.

Chapter 12. Attitude Scale Measurements Used in Marketing Research

a. 180SearchAssistant
c. Power III
b. 6-3-5 Brainwriting
d. Customer loyalty

29. _____ refer to a collection of facts usually collected as the result of experience, observation or experiment or a set of premises. This may consist of numbers, words particularly as measurements or observations of a set of variables. _____ are often viewed as a lowest level of abstraction from which information and knowledge are derived.

a. Mean
c. Pearson product-moment correlation coefficient
b. Data
d. Sample size

30. In statistics, an _____ is a term in a statistical model added when the effect of two or more variables is not simply additive. Such a term reflects that the effect of one variable depends on the values of one or more other variables.

Thus, for a response Y and two variables x_1 and x_2 an additive model would be:

$$Y = ax_1 + bx_2 + \text{error}$$

In contrast to this,

$$Y = ax_1 + bx_2 + c(x_1 \times x_2) + \text{error},$$

is an example of a model with an _____ between variables x_1 and x_2 ('error' refers to the random variable whose value by which y differs from the expected value of y.)

a. ACNielsen
c. ADTECH
b. AMAX
d. Interaction

31. _____ is a type of research conducted because a problem has not been clearly defined. _____ helps determine the best research design, data collection method and selection of subjects. Given its fundamental nature, _____ often concludes that a perceived problem does not actually exist.

a. ACNielsen
c. Intent scale translation
b. IDDEA
d. Exploratory research

32. _____ is a field of inquiry that crosscuts disciplines and subject matters. _____ers aim to gather an in-depth understanding of human behavior and the reasons that govern such behavior. The discipline investigates the why and how of decision making, not just what, where, when.

a. 6-3-5 Brainwriting
c. Qualitative research
b. Power III
d. 180SearchAssistant

33. A _____ attribute is one that exists in a range of magnitudes, and can therefore be measured. Measurements of any particular _____ property are expressed as a specific quantity, referred to as a unit, multiplied by a number. Examples of physical quantities are distance, mass, and time.

a. Dolly Dimples
c. Lifestyle city
b. BeyondROI
d. Quantitative

Chapter 12. Attitude Scale Measurements Used in Marketing Research

34. A number of different _____s are indicated below.

- Randomized controlled trial
    - Double-blind randomized trial
    - Single-blind randomized trial
    - Non-blind trial
- Nonrandomized trial (quasi-experiment)
    - Interrupted time series design (measures on a sample or a series of samples from the same population are obtained several times before and after a manipulated event or a naturally occurring event) - considered a type of quasi-experiment

- Cohort study
    - Prospective cohort
    - Retrospective cohort
    - Time series study
- Case-control study
    - Nested case-control study
- Cross-sectional study
    - Community survey (a type of cross-sectional study)

When choosing a _____, many factors must be taken into account. Different types of studies are subject to different types of bias. For example, recall bias is likely to occur in cross-sectional or case-control studies where subjects are asked to recall exposure to risk factors.

a. Study design
b. Longitudinal studies
c. 180SearchAssistant
d. Power III

Chapter 13. Questionnaire Design and Issues

1. A _____ is a research instrument consisting of a series of questions and other prompts for the purpose of gathering information from respondents. Although they are often designed for statistical analysis of the responses, this is not always the case. The _____ was invented by Sir Francis Galton.
   a. Questionnaire
   b. Mystery shopping
   c. Mystery shoppers
   d. Market research

2. A personal and cultural _____ is a relative ethic _____, an assumption upon which implementation can be extrapolated. A _____ system is a set of consistent _____s and measures that is soo not true. A principle _____ is a foundation upon which other _____s and measures of integrity are based.
   a. Perceptual maps
   b. Value
   c. Supreme Court of the United States
   d. Package-on-Package

3. _____ refer to a collection of facts usually collected as the result of experience, observation or experiment or a set of premises. This may consist of numbers, words particularly as measurements or observations of a set of variables. _____ are often viewed as a lowest level of abstraction from which information and knowledge are derived.
   a. Sample size
   b. Pearson product-moment correlation coefficient
   c. Mean
   d. Data

4. _____ is a term used to describe a process of preparing and collecting data - for example as part of a process improvement or similar project.

   _____ usually takes place early on in an improvement project, and is often formalised through a _____ Plan which often contains the following activity.

   1. Pre collection activity - Agree goals, target data, definitions, methods
   2. Collection - _____
   3. Present Findings - usually involves some form of sorting analysis and/or presentation.

   A formal _____ process is necessary as it ensures that data gathered is both defined and accurate and that subsequent decisions based on arguments embodied in the findings are valid . The process provides both a baseline from which to measure from and in certain cases a target on what to improve. Types of _____ 1-By mail questionnaires 2-By personal interview

   - Six sigma
   - Sampling (statistics)

   a. 180SearchAssistant
   b. 6-3-5 Brainwriting
   c. Data collection
   d. Power III

5. _____ is either an activity of a living being (such as a human), consisting of receiving knowledge of the outside world through the senses, or the recording of data using scientific instruments. The term may also refer to any datum collected during this activity.

The scientific method requires _____s of nature to formulate and test hypotheses.

a. ACNielsen
b. ADTECH
c. Observation
d. AMAX

6. The _____ and the null hypothesis are the two rival hypotheses whose likelihoods are compared by a statistical hypothesis test. Usually the _____ is the possibility that an observed effect is genuine and the null hypothesis is the rival possibility that it has resulted from chance.

The classical (or frequentist) approach is to calculate the probability that the observed effect (or one more extreme) will occur if the null hypothesis is true.

a. ACNielsen
b. Alternative hypothesis
c. Interval estimation
d. Analysis of variance

7. A _____ is a statement or claim that a particular event will occur in the future in more certain terms than a forecast. The etymology of this word is Latin . In regards to predicting the future Howard H. Stevenson Says, ' _____ is at least two things: Important and hard.' Important, because we have to act, and hard because we have to realize the future we want, and what is the best way to get there.

a. 180SearchAssistant
b. 6-3-5 Brainwriting
c. Power III
d. Prediction

8. A _____ is a structured collection of records or data that is stored in a computer system. The structure is achieved by organizing the data according to a _____ model. The model in most common use today is the relational model.

a. Database
b. 180SearchAssistant
c. Power III
d. 6-3-5 Brainwriting

9. In statistics, the _____ is a common measure of the correlation (linear dependence) between two variables X and Y. It is very widely used in the sciences as a measure of the strength of linear dependence between two variables, giving a value somewhere between +1 and -1 inclusive. It was first introduced by Francis Galton in the 1880s, and named after Karl Pearson.

In accordance with the usual convention, when calculated for an entire population, the Pearson product-moment correlation is typically designated by the analogous Greek letter, which in this case is ρ .

a. Pearson product-moment correlation coefficient
b. Standard deviation
c. Control chart
d. Median

10. A _____, in the field of business and marketing, is a geographic region or demographic group used to gauge the viability of a product or service in the mass market prior to a wide scale roll-out. The criteria used to judge the acceptability of a _____ region or group include:

1. a population that is demographically similar to the proposed target market; and
2. relative isolation from densely populated media markets so that advertising to the test audience can be efficient and economical.

The _____ ideally aims to duplicate 'everything' - promotion and distribution as well as `product' - on a smaller scale. The technique replicates, typically in one area, what is planned to occur in a national launch; and the results are very carefully monitored, so that they can be extrapolated to projected national results. The `area' may be any one of the following:

- Television area
- Test town
- Residential neighborhood
- Test site

A number of decisions have to be taken about any _____:

- Which _____?
- What is to be tested?
- How long a test?
- What are the success criteria?

The simple go or no-go decision, together with the related reduction of risk, is normally the main justification for the expense of _____s. At the same time, however, such _____s can be used to test specific elements of a new product's marketing mix; possibly the version of the product itself, the promotional message and media spend, the distribution channels and the price.

a. Power III
b. 180SearchAssistant
c. Preadolescence
d. Test market

11. An _____ is a special-purpose computer system designed to perform one or a few dedicated functions, often with real-time computing constraints. It is usually embedded as part of a complete device including hardware and mechanical parts. In contrast, a general-purpose computer, such as a personal computer, can do many different tasks depending on programming.

a. AMAX
b. ADTECH
c. ACNielsen
d. Embedded system

12. In probability theory and statistics, _____ indicates the strength and direction of a linear relationship between two random variables. That is in contrast with the usage of the term in colloquial speech, denoting any relationship, not necessarily linear. In general statistical usage, _____ or co-relation refers to the departure of two random variables from independence.

a. Correlation
b. Probability
c. Mean
d. Frequency distribution

13. _____ is a type of research conducted because a problem has not been clearly defined. _____ helps determine the best research design, data collection method and selection of subjects. Given its fundamental nature, _____ often concludes that a perceived problem does not actually exist.

a. Intent scale translation
c. ACNielsen
b. IDDEA
d. Exploratory research

14. _____ is defined by the American _____ Association as the activity, set of institutions, and processes for creating, communicating, delivering, and exchanging offerings that have value for customers, clients, partners, and society at large. The term developed from the original meaning which referred literally to going to market, as in shopping, or going to a market to sell goods or services.

_____ practice tends to be seen as a creative industry, which includes advertising, distribution and selling.

a. Customer acquisition management
c. Marketing
b. Product naming
d. Marketing myopia

15. In statistical hypothesis testing, the _____ formally describes some aspect of the statistical behaviour of a set of data; this description is treated as valid unless the actual behaviour of the data contradicts this assumption. Thus, the _____ is contrasted against another hypothesis. Statistical hypothesis testing is used to make a decision about whether the data contradicts the _____: this is called significance testing.

a. Variance
c. Statistical hypothesis test
b. Standard score
d. Null hypothesis

16. A number of different _____s are indicated below.

- Randomized controlled trial
    - Double-blind randomized trial
    - Single-blind randomized trial
    - Non-blind trial
- Nonrandomized trial (quasi-experiment)
    - Interrupted time series design (measures on a sample or a series of samples from the same population are obtained several times before and after a manipulated event or a naturally occurring event) - considered a type of quasi-experiment

- Cohort study
    - Prospective cohort
    - Retrospective cohort
    - Time series study
- Case-control study
    - Nested case-control study
- Cross-sectional study
    - Community survey (a type of cross-sectional study)

When choosing a _____, many factors must be taken into account. Different types of studies are subject to different types of bias. For example, recall bias is likely to occur in cross-sectional or case-control studies where subjects are asked to recall exposure to risk factors.

a. Study design
b. 180SearchAssistant
c. Longitudinal studies
d. Power III

17. _____ or _____ data refers to selected population characteristics as used in government, marketing or opinion research, or the _____ profiles used in such research. Note the distinction from the term 'demography' Commonly-used _____ include race, age, income, disabilities, mobility (in terms of travel time to work or number of vehicles available), educational attainment, home ownership, employment status, and even location.

a. Albert Einstein
b. Demographic
c. AStore
d. African Americans

18. _____ is systematic determination of merit, worth, and significance of something or someone using criteria against a set of standards. _____ often is used to characterize and appraise subjects of interest in a wide range of human enterprises, including the arts, criminal justice, foundations and non-profit organizations, government, health care, and other human services.

Depending on the topic of interest, there are professional groups which look to the quality and rigor of the _____ process.

a. AMAX
b. ACNielsen
c. ADTECH
d. Evaluation

19. _____ is the realization of an application idea, model, design, specification, standard, algorithm an _____ is a realization of a technical specification or algorithm as a program, software component, or other computer system. Many _____s may exist for a given specification or standard.

a. AMAX
b. ADTECH
c. ACNielsen
d. Implementation

20. _____ has been defined by the International Organization for Standardization (ISO) as 'ensuring that information is accessible only to those authorized to have access' and is one of the cornerstones of information security. _____ is one of the design goals for many cryptosystems, made possible in practice by the techniques of modern cryptography.

_____ also refers to an ethical principle associated with several professions (e.g., medicine, law, religion, professional psychology, and journalism.)

a. Confidentiality
b. Power III
c. 6-3-5 Brainwriting
d. 180SearchAssistant

21. _____ or personalisation is tailoring a consumer product, electronic or written medium to a user based on personal details or characteristics they provide. More recently, it has especially been applied in the context of the World Wide Web.

Web pages are personalized based on the interests of an individual.

a. Sexism,
b. Complex sale
c. Flighting
d. Personalization

Chapter 13. Questionnaire Design and Issues 131

22. In operant conditioning, _____ occurs when an event following a response causes an increase in the probability of that response occurring in the future. Response strength can be assessed by measures such as the frequency with which the response is made (for example, a pigeon may peck a key more times in the session), or the speed with which it is made (for example, a rat may run a maze faster.) The environment change contingent upon the response is called a reinforcer.
 a. Generic brands
 b. Reinforcement
 c. Relationship Management Application
 d. Completely randomized designs

23. In economics and sociology, an _____ is any factor (financial or non-financial) that enables or motivates a particular course of action, or counts as a reason for preferring one choice to the alternatives. It is an expectation that encourages people to behave in a certain way. Since human beings are purposeful creatures, the study of _____ structures is central to the study of all economic activity (both in terms of individual decision-making and in terms of co-operation and competition within a larger institutional structure.)
 a. ADTECH
 b. ACNielsen
 c. AMAX
 d. Incentive

24. Consumer market research is a form of applied sociology that concentrates on understanding the behaviours, whims and preferences, of consumers in a market-based economy, and aims to understand the effects and comparative success of marketing campaigns. The field of consumer _____ as a statistical science was pioneered by Arthur Nielsen with the founding of the ACNielsen Company in 1923 .

Thus _____ is the systematic and objective identification, collection, analysis, and dissemination of information for the purpose of assisting management in decision making related to the identification and solution of problems and opportunities in marketing.

 a. Marketing research process
 b. Logit analysis
 c. Marketing research
 d. Focus group

25. The _____ is a professional association for marketers. As of 2008 it had approximately 40,000 members. There are collegiate chapters on 250 campuses.
 a. ADTECH
 b. ACNielsen
 c. American Marketing Association
 d. AMAX

26. _____ is a branch of philosophy which seeks to address questions about morality, such as how a moral outcome can be achieved in a specific situation (applied _____), how moral values should be determined (normative _____), what moral values people actually abide by (descriptive _____), what the fundamental semantic, ontological, and epistemic nature of _____ or morality is (meta-_____), and how moral capacity or moral agency develops and what its nature is (moral psychology.)

Socrates was one of the first Greek philosophers to encourage both scholars and the common citizen to turn their attention from the outside world to the condition of man. In this view, Knowledge having a bearing on human life was placed highest, all other knowledge being secondary.

 a. AMAX
 b. ADTECH
 c. ACNielsen
 d. Ethics

27. _____ is the ability of an individual or group to seclude themselves or information about themselves and thereby reveal themselves selectively. The boundaries and content of what is considered private differ among cultures and individuals, but share basic common themes. _____ is sometimes related to anonymity, the wish to remain unnoticed or unidentified in the public realm.

   a. Power III
   b. 180SearchAssistant
   c. 6-3-5 Brainwriting
   d. Privacy

28. A _____ is a psychometric scale commonly used in questionnaires, and is the most widely used scale in survey research. When responding to a Likert questionnaire item, respondents specify their level of agreement to a statement. The scale is named after its inventor, psychologist Rensis Likert.

   a. Semantic differential
   b. Factor analysis
   c. Likert scale
   d. Power III

Chapter 14. Coding, Editing, and Preparing Data for Analysis

1. _____ refer to a collection of facts usually collected as the result of experience, observation or experiment or a set of premises. This may consist of numbers, words particularly as measurements or observations of a set of variables. _____ are often viewed as a lowest level of abstraction from which information and knowledge are derived.
   a. Sample size
   b. Mean
   c. Pearson product-moment correlation coefficient
   d. Data

2. A personal and cultural _____ is a relative ethic _____, an assumption upon which implementation can be extrapolated. A _____ system is a set of consistent _____s and measures that is soo not true. A principle _____ is a foundation upon which other _____s and measures of integrity are based.
   a. Supreme Court of the United States
   b. Package-on-Package
   c. Perceptual maps
   d. Value

3. _____ is a type of research conducted because a problem has not been clearly defined. _____ helps determine the best research design, data collection method and selection of subjects. Given its fundamental nature, _____ often concludes that a perceived problem does not actually exist.
   a. Exploratory research
   b. Intent scale translation
   c. ACNielsen
   d. IDDEA

4. A number of different _____s are indicated below.

   - Randomized controlled trial
     - Double-blind randomized trial
     - Single-blind randomized trial
     - Non-blind trial
   - Nonrandomized trial (quasi-experiment)
     - Interrupted time series design (measures on a sample or a series of samples from the same population are obtained several times before and after a manipulated event or a naturally occurring event) - considered a type of quasi-experiment

   - Cohort study
     - Prospective cohort
     - Retrospective cohort
     - Time series study
   - Case-control study
     - Nested case-control study
   - Cross-sectional study
     - Community survey (a type of cross-sectional study)

   When choosing a _____, many factors must be taken into account. Different types of studies are subject to different types of bias. For example, recall bias is likely to occur in cross-sectional or case-control studies where subjects are asked to recall exposure to risk factors.

   a. Power III
   b. Study design
   c. Longitudinal studies
   d. 180SearchAssistant

Chapter 14. Coding, Editing, and Preparing Data for Analysis

5. In statistics, the _____ is a common measure of the correlation (linear dependence) between two variables X and Y. It is very widely used in the sciences as a measure of the strength of linear dependence between two variables, giving a value somewhere between +1 and -1 inclusive. It was first introduced by Francis Galton in the 1880s, and named after Karl Pearson.

In accordance with the usual convention, when calculated for an entire population, the Pearson product-moment correlation is typically designated by the analogous Greek letter, which in this case is ρ .

   a. Pearson product-moment correlation coefficient
   b. Median
   c. Control chart
   d. Standard deviation

6. In probability theory and statistics, _____ indicates the strength and direction of a linear relationship between two random variables. That is in contrast with the usage of the term in colloquial speech, denoting any relationship, not necessarily linear. In general statistical usage, _____ or co-relation refers to the departure of two random variables from independence.
   a. Correlation
   b. Mean
   c. Probability
   d. Frequency distribution

7. A _____ is a research instrument consisting of a series of questions and other prompts for the purpose of gathering information from respondents. Although they are often designed for statistical analysis of the responses, this is not always the case. The _____ was invented by Sir Francis Galton.
   a. Market research
   b. Questionnaire
   c. Mystery shopping
   d. Mystery shoppers

8. _____ is a computer program used for statistical analysis.

_____ (originally, Statistical Package for the Social Sciences) was released in its first version in 1968 after being founded by Norman Nie and C. Hadlai Hull. Nie was then a political science postgraduate at Stanford University,and now Research Professor in the Department of Political Science at Stanford and Professor Emeritus of Political Science at the University of Chicago.

   a. Power III
   b. 180SearchAssistant
   c. 6-3-5 Brainwriting
   d. SPSS

9. _____ is a process of gathering, modeling, and transforming data with the goal of highlighting useful information, suggesting conclusions, and supporting decision making. _____ has multiple facets and approaches, encompassing diverse techniques under a variety of names, in different business, science, and social science domains.

Data mining is a particular _____ technique that focuses on modeling and knowledge discovery for predictive rather than purely descriptive purposes.

   a. 6-3-5 Brainwriting
   b. Data analysis
   c. Power III
   d. 180SearchAssistant

Chapter 14. Coding, Editing, and Preparing Data for Analysis

10. _____s are used in open sentences. For instance, in the formula x + 1 = 5, x is a _____ which represents an 'unknown' number. _____s are often represented by letters of the Roman alphabet, or those of other alphabets, such as Greek, and use other special symbols.
   a. Variable
   b. Book of business
   c. Personalization
   d. Quantitative

11. _____ are used to collect quantitative information about items in a population. Surveys of human populations and institutions are common in political polling and government, health, social science and marketing research. A survey may focus on opinions or factual information depending on its purpose, and many surveys involve administering questions to individuals.
   a. BeyondROI
   b. Gross Margin Return on Inventory Investment
   c. Convergent
   d. Statistical surveys

12. _____ is a concept that denotes the precise probability of specific eventualities. Technically, the notion of _____ is independent from the notion of value and, as such, eventualities may have both beneficial and adverse consequences. However, in general usage the convention is to focus only on potential negative impact to some characteristic of value that may arise from a future event.
   a. 6-3-5 Brainwriting
   b. Power III
   c. 180SearchAssistant
   d. Risk

13. _____ is a mathematical science pertaining to the collection, analysis, interpretation or explanation, and presentation of data. It also provides tools for prediction and forecasting based on data. It is applicable to a wide variety of academic disciplines, from the natural and social sciences to the humanities, government and business.
   a. Median
   b. Null hypothesis
   c. Type I error
   d. Statistics

14. _____ are used to describe the basic features of the data gathered from an experimental study in various ways. A _____ is distinguished from inductive statistics. They provide simple summaries about the sample and the measures.
   a. Descriptive statistics
   b. P-Value
   c. Frequency distribution
   d. Pearson product-moment correlation coefficient

15. In statistics, _____ has two related meanings:

   - the arithmetic _____
   - the expected value of a random variable, which is also called the population _____.

   It is sometimes stated that the '_____' _____s average. This is incorrect if '_____' is taken in the specific sense of 'arithmetic _____' as there are different types of averages: the _____, median, and mode. For instance, average house prices almost always use the median value for the average. These three types of averages are all measures of locations.

   a. Heteroskedastic
   b. Standard normal distribution
   c. Confidence interval
   d. Mean

16. In probability theory and statistics, a _____ is described as the number separating the higher half of a sample, a population from the lower half. The _____ of a finite list of numbers can be found by arranging all the observations from lowest value to highest value and picking the middle one. If there is an even number of observations, the _____ is not unique, so one often takes the mean of the two middle values.

   a. Frequency distribution
   b. Statistically significant
   c. Linear regression
   d. Median

17. _____ is the process of making something random; this means:

- Generating a random permutation of a sequence (such as when shuffling cards.)
- Selecting a random sample of a population (important in statistical sampling.)
- Generating random numbers: see Random number generation.
- Transforming a data stream using a scrambler in telecommunications.

_____ is used extensively in the field of gambling (or generally being random.) Imperfect _____ may allow a skilled gambler to have an advantage, so much research has been devoted to effective _____. A classic example of _____ is shuffling playing cards.

_____ is a core principle in the statistical theory of design of experiments.

   a. Sample size
   b. Statistics
   c. Randomization
   d. Standard deviation

18. In statistics, _____ is a simple measure of the variability or dispersion of a data set. A low _____ indicates that the data points tend to be very close to the same value (the mean), while high _____ indicates that the data are 'spread out' over a large range of values.

For example, the average height for adult men in the United States is about 70 inches, with a _____ of around 3 inches.

   a. Z-test
   b. Pearson product-moment correlation coefficient
   c. Statistically significant
   d. Standard deviation

19. In mathematics, an _____, or central tendency of a data set refers to a measure of the 'middle' or 'expected' value of the data set. There are many different descriptive statistics that can be chosen as a measurement of the central tendency of the data items.

An _____ is a single value that is meant to typify a list of values.

   a. ADTECH
   b. AMAX
   c. Average
   d. ACNielsen

20. _____ is the process of extracting hidden patterns from data. As more data is gathered, with the amount of data doubling every three years, _____ is becoming an increasingly important tool to transform this data into information. It is commonly used in a wide range of profiling practices, such as marketing, surveillance, fraud detection and scientific discovery.

a. Power III
b. 180SearchAssistant
c. Structure mining
d. Data mining

21. A _____ is a structured collection of records or data that is stored in a computer system. The structure is achieved by organizing the data according to a _____ model. The model in most common use today is the relational model.
   a. 6-3-5 Brainwriting
   b. Power III
   c. 180SearchAssistant
   d. Database

22. In psychology, philosophy, and the cognitive sciences, _____ is the process of attaining awareness or understanding of sensory information. It is a task far more complex than was imagined in the 1950s and 1960s, when it was predicted that building perceiving machines would take about a decade, a goal which is still very far from fruition. The word _____ comes from the Latin words _____, percepio, meaning 'receiving, collecting, action of taking possession, apprehension with the mind or senses.'

_____ is one of the oldest fields in psychology.

   a. 180SearchAssistant
   b. Groupthink
   c. Perception
   d. Power III

Chapter 15. Data Analysis: Testing for Significant Differences

1. _____ is a computer program used for statistical analysis.

_____ (originally, Statistical Package for the Social Sciences) was released in its first version in 1968 after being founded by Norman Nie and C. Hadlai Hull. Nie was then a political science postgraduate at Stanford University, and now Research Professor in the Department of Political Science at Stanford and Professor Emeritus of Political Science at the University of Chicago.

   a. Power III
   c. 180SearchAssistant
   b. 6-3-5 Brainwriting
   d. SPSS

2. The _____ and the null hypothesis are the two rival hypotheses whose likelihoods are compared by a statistical hypothesis test. Usually the _____ is the possibility that an observed effect is genuine and the null hypothesis is the rival possibility that it has resulted from chance.

The classical (or frequentist) approach is to calculate the probability that the observed effect (or one more extreme) will occur if the null hypothesis is true.

   a. ACNielsen
   c. Alternative hypothesis
   b. Analysis of variance
   d. Interval estimation

3. _____ refer to a collection of facts usually collected as the result of experience, observation or experiment or a set of premises. This may consist of numbers, words particularly as measurements or observations of a set of variables. _____ are often viewed as a lowest level of abstraction from which information and knowledge are derived.

   a. Sample size
   c. Mean
   b. Data
   d. Pearson product-moment correlation coefficient

4. _____ are used to describe the basic features of the data gathered from an experimental study in various ways. A _____ is distinguished from inductive statistics. They provide simple summaries about the sample and the measures.

   a. P-Value
   c. Frequency distribution
   b. Descriptive statistics
   d. Pearson product-moment correlation coefficient

5. _____ is one of the four elements of marketing mix. An organization or set of organizations (go-betweens) involved in the process of making a product or service available for use or consumption by a consumer or business user.

The other three parts of the marketing mix are product, pricing, and promotion.

   a. Better Living Through Chemistry
   c. Japan Advertising Photographers' Association
   b. Comparison-Shopping agent
   d. Distribution

6. In statistics, a _____ is a tabulation of the values that one or more variables take in a sample.

Univariate _____s are often presented as lists, ordered by quantity, showing the number of times each value appears. For example, if 100 people rate a five-point Likert scale assessing their agreement with a statement on a scale on which 1 denotes strong agreement and 5 strong disagreement, the _____ of their responses might look like:

This simple tabulation has two drawbacks.

a. Survey research
b. Statistics
c. Frequency distribution
d. Confidence interval

7. _____ is a mathematical science pertaining to the collection, analysis, interpretation or explanation, and presentation of data. It also provides tools for prediction and forecasting based on data. It is applicable to a wide variety of academic disciplines, from the natural and social sciences to the humanities, government and business.

a. Median
b. Type I error
c. Null hypothesis
d. Statistics

8. A personal and cultural _____ is a relative ethic _____, an assumption upon which implementation can be extrapolated. A _____ system is a set of consistent _____s and measures that is soo not true. A principle _____ is a foundation upon which other _____s and measures of integrity are based.

a. Perceptual maps
b. Value
c. Supreme Court of the United States
d. Package-on-Package

9. In statistics, _____ has two related meanings:

- the arithmetic _____
- the expected value of a random variable, which is also called the population _____.

It is sometimes stated that the '_____' _____s average. This is incorrect if '_____' is taken in the specific sense of 'arithmetic _____' as there are different types of averages: the _____, median, and mode. For instance, average house prices almost always use the median value for the average. These three types of averages are all measures of locations.

a. Heteroskedastic
b. Standard normal distribution
c. Confidence interval
d. Mean

10. In probability theory and statistics, a _____ is described as the number separating the higher half of a sample, a population from the lower half. The _____ of a finite list of numbers can be found by arranging all the observations from lowest value to highest value and picking the middle one. If there is an even number of observations, the _____ is not unique, so one often takes the mean of the two middle values.

a. Median
b. Statistically significant
c. Linear regression
d. Frequency distribution

11. The '_____' is an expression which typically refers to the theory of scale types developed by the Harvard psychologist Stanley Smith Stevens In this article Stevens claimed that all measurement in science was conducted using four different types of numerical scales which he called 'nominal', 'ordinal', 'interval' and 'ratio'.

a. 180SearchAssistant
b. Power III
c. 6-3-5 Brainwriting
d. Levels of measurement

Chapter 15. Data Analysis: Testing for Significant Differences

12. _____ is the process of making something random; this means:

- Generating a random permutation of a sequence (such as when shuffling cards.)
- Selecting a random sample of a population (important in statistical sampling.)
- Generating random numbers: see Random number generation.
- Transforming a data stream using a scrambler in telecommunications.

_____ is used extensively in the field of gambling (or generally being random.) Imperfect _____ may allow a skilled gambler to have an advantage, so much research has been devoted to effective _____. A classic example of _____ is shuffling playing cards.

_____ is a core principle in the statistical theory of design of experiments.

a. Randomization
c. Sample size
b. Statistics
d. Standard deviation

13. In mathematics, an _____, or central tendency of a data set refers to a measure of the 'middle' or 'expected' value of the data set. There are many different descriptive statistics that can be chosen as a measurement of the central tendency of the data items.

An _____ is a single value that is meant to typify a list of values.

a. AMAX
c. ADTECH
b. ACNielsen
d. Average

14. In descriptive statistics, the _____ is the length of the smallest interval which contains all the data. It is calculated by subtracting the smallest observation (sample minimum) from the greatest (sample maximum) and provides an indication of statistical dispersion.

It is measured in the same units as the data.

a. Personalization
c. Just-In-Case
b. Range
d. Japan Advertising Photographers' Association

15. In statistics, the _____ is a common measure of the correlation (linear dependence) between two variables X and Y. It is very widely used in the sciences as a measure of the strength of linear dependence between two variables, giving a value somewhere between +1 and -1 inclusive. It was first introduced by Francis Galton in the 1880s, and named after Karl Pearson.

In accordance with the usual convention, when calculated for an entire population, the Pearson product-moment correlation is typically designated by the analogous Greek letter, which in this case is ρ .

a. Control chart
c. Median
b. Standard deviation
d. Pearson product-moment correlation coefficient

Chapter 15. Data Analysis: Testing for Significant Differences

16. In statistics, _____ is a simple measure of the variability or dispersion of a data set. A low _____ indicates that the data points tend to be very close to the same value (the mean), while high _____ indicates that the data are 'spread out' over a large range of values.

For example, the average height for adult men in the United States is about 70 inches, with a _____ of around 3 inches.

   a. Z-test   b. Statistically significant
   c. Pearson product-moment correlation coefficient   d. Standard deviation

17. _____s are used in open sentences. For instance, in the formula x + 1 = 5, x is a _____ which represents an 'unknown' number. _____s are often represented by letters of the Roman alphabet, or those of other alphabets, such as Greek, and use other special symbols.
   a. Personalization   b. Quantitative
   c. Book of business   d. Variable

18. In probability theory and statistics, the _____ of a random variable, probability distribution, or sample is a measure of statistical dispersion, averaging the squared distance of its possible values from the expected value (mean.) Whereas the mean is a way to describe the location of a distribution, the _____ is a way to capture its scale or degree of being spread out. The unit of _____ is the square of the unit of the original variable.
   a. Sample size   b. Correlation
   c. Variance   d. Standard deviation

19. In probability theory and statistics, _____ indicates the strength and direction of a linear relationship between two random variables. That is in contrast with the usage of the term in colloquial speech, denoting any relationship, not necessarily linear. In general statistical usage, _____ or co-relation refers to the departure of two random variables from independence.
   a. Mean   b. Frequency distribution
   c. Probability   d. Correlation

20. An example of a repeated measures _____ would be if one group were pre- and post-tested. (This example occurs in education quite frequently.) If a teacher wanted to examine the effect of a new set of textbooks on student achievement, (s)he could test the class at the beginning of the year (pretest) and at the end of the year (posttest.)
   a. Statistically significant   b. Moving average
   c. T-test   d. Null hypothesis

21. _____ is a statistical phenomenon in which two or more predictor variables in a multiple regression model are highly correlated. In this situation the coefficient estimates may change erratically in response to small changes in the model or the data. _____ does not reduce the predictive power or reliability of the model as a whole; it only affects calculations regarding individual predictors.
   a. Regression analysis   b. Variance inflation factor
   c. Multicollinearity   d. Stepwise regression

22. In statistics, _____ is used for two things;

- to construct a simple formula that will predict what value will occur for a quantity of interest when other related variables take given values.
- to allow a test to be made of whether a given variable does have an effect on a quantity of interest in situations where there may be many related variables.

In both cases, several sets of outcomes are available for the quantity of interest together with the related variables.

_____ is a form of regression analysis in which the relationship between one or more independent variables and another variable, called the dependent variable, is modelled by a least squares function, called a _____ equation. This function is a linear combination of one or more model parameters, called regression coefficients. A _____ equation with one independent variable represents a straight line when the predicted value (i.e. the dependant variable from the regression equation) is plotted against the independent variable: this is called a simple _____.

    a. Heteroskedastic
    c. Sample size
    b. Descriptive statistics
    d. Linear regression

23. In statistical hypothesis testing, the _____ formally describes some aspect of the statistical behaviour of a set of data; this description is treated as valid unless the actual behaviour of the data contradicts this assumption. Thus, the _____ is contrasted against another hypothesis. Statistical hypothesis testing is used to make a decision about whether the data contradicts the _____: this is called significance testing.

    a. Standard score
    c. Null hypothesis
    b. Statistical hypothesis test
    d. Variance

24. In statistics, _____ is a collective name for techniques for the modeling and analysis of numerical data consisting of values of a dependent variable and of one or more independent variables The dependent variable in the regression equation is modeled as a function of the independent variables, corresponding parameters, and an error term. The error term is treated as a random variable.

    a. Multicollinearity
    c. Variance inflation factor
    b. Stepwise regression
    d. Regression analysis

25. In statistics, the terms _____ and type II error are used to describe possible errors made in a statistical decision process. In 1928, Jerzy Neyman (1894-1981) and Egon Pearson (1895-1980), both eminent statisticians, discussed the problems associated with 'deciding whether or not a particular sample may be judged as likely to have been randomly drawn from a certain population' (1928/1967, p.1): and identified 'two sources of error', namely:

    Type I ($>\alpha$): reject the null-hypothesis when the null-hypothesis is true, and
    Type II ($>\beta$): fail to reject the null-hypothesis when the null-hypothesis is false

In 1930, they elaborated on these two sources of error, remarking that 'in testing hypotheses two considerations must be kept in view, (1) we must be able to reduce the chance of rejecting a true hypothesis to as low a value as desired; (2) the test must be so devised that it will reject the hypothesis tested when it is likely to be false'

Chapter 15. Data Analysis: Testing for Significant Differences 143

Scientists recognize two different sorts of error:

- Statistical error: the difference between a computed, estimated specified and inherently unpredictable fluctuations in the measurement apparatus or the system being studied.
- Systematic error: the difference between a computed, estimated specified and which, once identified, can usually be eliminated.

Statisticians speak of two significant sorts of statistical error. The context is that there is a 'null hypothesis' which corresponds to a presumed default 'state of nature', e.g., that an individual is free of disease, that an accused is innocent that is, that the individual has the disease, that the accused is guilty, or that the login candidate is an authorized user.

    a. Probability sampling   b. Type I error
    c. Mean   d. Significance level

26. _____ is a process of gathering, modeling, and transforming data with the goal of highlighting useful information, suggesting conclusions, and supporting decision making. _____ has multiple facets and approaches, encompassing diverse techniques under a variety of names, in different business, science, and social science domains.

Data mining is a particular _____ technique that focuses on modeling and knowledge discovery for predictive rather than purely descriptive purposes.

    a. 180SearchAssistant   b. Data analysis
    c. 6-3-5 Brainwriting   d. Power III

27. 'Speaking generally, properties are those physical quantities which directly describe the physical attributes of the system; _____s are those combinations of the properties which suffice to determine the response of the system. Properties can have all sorts of dimensions, depending upon the system being considered; _____s are dimensionless, or have the dimension of time or its reciprocal.'

The term can also be used in engineering contexts, however, as it is typically used in the physical sciences.

When the terms formal _____ and actual _____ are used, they generally correspond with the definitions used in computer science.

    a. 6-3-5 Brainwriting   b. 180SearchAssistant
    c. Power III   d. Parameter

28. The _____ of a statistical sample is the number of observations that constitute it. It is typically denoted n, a positive integer (natural number.)

Typically, all else being equal, a larger _____ leads to increased precision in estimates of various properties of the population.

a. Data
b. Heteroskedastic
c. Frequency distribution
d. Sample size

29. In statistics, a result is called _____ if it is unlikely to have occurred by chance. 'A _____ difference' simply means there is statistical evidence that there is a difference; it does not mean the difference is necessarily large, important, or significant in the common meaning of the word.

The significance level of a test is a traditional frequentist statistical hypothesis testing concept.

a. Frequency distribution
b. Randomization
c. Standard deviation
d. Statistically significant

30. A _____ is any statistical test for which the distribution of the test statistic under the null hypothesis can be approximated by a normal distribution. Since many test statistics are approximately normally distributed for large samples (due to the central limit theorem), many statistical tests can be performed as approximate _____ s if the sample size is not too small. In addition, some statistical tests such as comparisons of means between two samples, or a comparison of the mean of one sample to a given constant, are exact _____ s under certain assumptions.

a. Confounding variables
b. Sample size
c. Z-test
d. Null hypothesis

31. The _____ is a professional association for marketers. As of 2008 it had approximately 40,000 members. There are collegiate chapters on 250 campuses.

a. American Marketing Association
b. ACNielsen
c. AMAX
d. ADTECH

32. _____ is a branch of philosophy which seeks to address questions about morality, such as how a moral outcome can be achieved in a specific situation (applied _____), how moral values should be determined (normative _____), what moral values people actually abide by (descriptive _____), what the fundamental semantic, ontological, and epistemic nature of _____ or morality is (meta-_____), and how moral capacity or moral agency develops and what its nature is (moral psychology.)

Socrates was one of the first Greek philosophers to encourage both scholars and the common citizen to turn their attention from the outside world to the condition of man. In this view, Knowledge having a bearing on human life was placed highest, all other knowledge being secondary.

a. AMAX
b. ACNielsen
c. ADTECH
d. Ethics

33. _____ is defined by the American _____ Association as the activity, set of institutions, and processes for creating, communicating, delivering, and exchanging offerings that have value for customers, clients, partners, and society at large. The term developed from the original meaning which referred literally to going to market, as in shopping, or going to a market to sell goods or services.

_____ practice tends to be seen as a creative industry, which includes advertising, distribution and selling.

Chapter 15. Data Analysis: Testing for Significant Differences

a. Marketing myopia
b. Customer acquisition management
c. Product naming
d. Marketing

34. Consumer market research is a form of applied sociology that concentrates on understanding the behaviours, whims and preferences, of consumers in a market-based economy, and aims to understand the effects and comparative success of marketing campaigns. The field of consumer _____ as a statistical science was pioneered by Arthur Nielsen with the founding of the ACNielsen Company in 1923.

Thus _____ is the systematic and objective identification, collection, analysis, and dissemination of information for the purpose of assisting management in decision making related to the identification and solution of problems and opportunities in marketing.

a. Marketing Research
b. Marketing research process
c. Focus group
d. Logit analysis

35. _____ is the ability of an individual or group to seclude themselves or information about themselves and thereby reveal themselves selectively. The boundaries and content of what is considered private differ among cultures and individuals, but share basic common themes. _____ is sometimes related to anonymity, the wish to remain unnoticed or unidentified in the public realm.

a. Power III
b. 6-3-5 Brainwriting
c. 180SearchAssistant
d. Privacy

36. In statistics, _____ is a collection of statistical models, and their associated procedures, in which the observed variance is partitioned into components due to different explanatory variables. The initial techniques of the _____ were developed by the statistician and geneticist R. A. Fisher in the 1920s and 1930s, and is sometimes known as Fisher's ANOVA or Fisher's _____, due to the use of Fisher's F-distribution as part of the test of statistical significance.

There are three conceptual classes of such models:

1. Fixed-effects models assumes that the data came from normal populations which may differ only in their means. (Model 1)
2. Random effects models assume that the data describe a hierarchy of different populations whose differences are constrained by the hierarchy. (Model 2)
3. Mixed-effect models describe situations where both fixed and random effects are present. (Model 3)

In practice, there are several types of ANOVA depending on the number of treatments and the way they are applied to the subjects in the experiment:

- One-way ANOVA is used to test for differences among two or more independent groups. Typically, however, the One-way ANOVA is used to test for differences among at least three groups, since the two-group case can be covered by a T-test (Gossett, 1908.)

a. Interval estimation
b. Arithmetic mean
c. ACNielsen
d. Analysis of variance

Chapter 15. Data Analysis: Testing for Significant Differences

37. Mystery shopping or Mystery Consumer is a tool used by market research companies to measure quality of retail service or gather specific information about products and services. _____ posing as normal customers perform specific tasks-- such as purchasing a product, asking questions, registering complaints or behaving in a certain way - and then provide detailed reports or feedback about their experiences.

Mystery shopping began in the 1940s as a way to measure employee integrity.

a. Questionnaire
c. Mystery shopping
b. Market research
d. Mystery shoppers

38. _____ is a graphics technique used by asset marketers that attempts to visually display the perceptions of customers or potential customers. Typically the position of a product, product line, brand, or company is displayed relative to their competition.

Perceptual maps can have any number of dimensions but the most common is two dimensions.

a. Market environment
c. Customer franchise
b. Kano model
d. Perceptual mapping

39. In marketing, _____ has come to mean the process by which marketers try to create an image or identity in the minds of their target market for its product, brand, or organization. It is the 'relative competitive comparison' their product occupies in a given market as perceived by the target market.

Re-_____ involves changing the identity of a product, relative to the identity of competing products, in the collective minds of the target market.

a. Moratorium
c. Containerization
b. GE matrix
d. Positioning

40. _____ is a form of communication that typically attempts to persuade potential customers to purchase or to consume more of a particular brand of product or service. 'While now central to the contemporary global economy and the reproduction of global production networks, it is only quite recently that _____ has been more than a marginal influence on patterns of sales and production. The formation of modern _____ was intimately bound up with the emergence of new forms of monopoly capitalism around the end of the 19th and beginning of the 20th century as one element in corporate strategies to create, organize and where possible control markets, especially for mass produced consumer goods.

a. Advertising
c. ACNielsen
b. AMAX
d. ADTECH

41. _____ in organizations and public policy is both the organizational process of creating and maintaining a plan; and the psychological process of thinking about the activities required to create a desired goal on some scale. As such, it is a fundamental property of intelligent behavior. This thought process is essential to the creation and refinement of a plan, or integration of it with other plans, that is, it combines forecasting of developments with the preparation of scenarios of how to react to them.

a. 180SearchAssistant
c. Power III
b. 6-3-5 Brainwriting
d. Planning

Chapter 15. Data Analysis: Testing for Significant Differences   147

42. _____ is an American firm that measures media audiences, including television, radio, theatre films (via the AMC MAP program) and newspapers. _____, headquartered in New York City and operating primarily from Chicago, is best-known for the Nielsen Ratings, a measurement of television viewership.

_____, the preeminent media research company in the world, began as a division of ACNielsen, a marketing research firm.

a. CoolBrands
b. Hennes ' Mauritz
c. Green Earth Market
d. Nielsen Media Research

43. A _____ is a research instrument consisting of a series of questions and other prompts for the purpose of gathering information from respondents. Although they are often designed for statistical analysis of the responses, this is not always the case. The _____ was invented by Sir Francis Galton.

a. Mystery shopping
b. Market research
c. Mystery shoppers
d. Questionnaire

Chapter 16. Data Analysis: Testing for Association

1. _____ is defined by the American _____ Association as the activity, set of institutions, and processes for creating, communicating, delivering, and exchanging offerings that have value for customers, clients, partners, and society at large. The term developed from the original meaning which referred literally to going to market, as in shopping, or going to a market to sell goods or services.

_____ practice tends to be seen as a creative industry, which includes advertising, distribution and selling.

   a. Product naming
   b. Marketing myopia
   c. Customer acquisition management
   d. Marketing

2. _____ is the term used to describe a situation where different entities cooperate advantageously for a final outcome. Simply defined, it means that the whole is greater than the sum of its parts. The essence of _____ is to value differences.
   a. 6-3-5 Brainwriting
   b. Synergy
   c. Power III
   d. 180SearchAssistant

3. In probability theory and statistics, _____ indicates the strength and direction of a linear relationship between two random variables. That is in contrast with the usage of the term in colloquial speech, denoting any relationship, not necessarily linear. In general statistical usage, _____ or co-relation refers to the departure of two random variables from independence.
   a. Mean
   b. Correlation
   c. Probability
   d. Frequency distribution

4. In statistics, the _____ is a common measure of the correlation (linear dependence) between two variables X and Y. It is very widely used in the sciences as a measure of the strength of linear dependence between two variables, giving a value somewhere between +1 and -1 inclusive. It was first introduced by Francis Galton in the 1880s, and named after Karl Pearson.

In accordance with the usual convention, when calculated for an entire population, the Pearson product-moment correlation is typically designated by the analogous Greek letter, which in this case is ρ .

   a. Pearson product-moment correlation coefficient
   b. Standard deviation
   c. Control chart
   d. Median

5. In statistics, _____ is a collective name for techniques for the modeling and analysis of numerical data consisting of values of a dependent variable and of one or more independent variables The dependent variable in the regression equation is modeled as a function of the independent variables, corresponding parameters, and an error term. The error term is treated as a random variable.
   a. Variance inflation factor
   b. Stepwise regression
   c. Regression analysis
   d. Multicollinearity

6. In statistics, a result is called _____ if it is unlikely to have occurred by chance. 'A _____ difference' simply means there is statistical evidence that there is a difference; it does not mean the difference is necessarily large, important, or significant in the common meaning of the word.

The significance level of a test is a traditional frequentist statistical hypothesis testing concept.

a. Frequency distribution
b. Standard deviation
c. Randomization
d. Statistically significant

7. _____s are used in open sentences. For instance, in the formula x + 1 = 5, x is a _____ which represents an 'unknown' number. _____s are often represented by letters of the Roman alphabet, or those of other alphabets, such as Greek, and use other special symbols.
   a. Book of business
   b. Personalization
   c. Quantitative
   d. Variable

8. A personal and cultural _____ is a relative ethic _____, an assumption upon which implementation can be extrapolated. A _____ system is a set of consistent _____s and measures that is soo not true. A principle _____ is a foundation upon which other _____s and measures of integrity are based.
   a. Package-on-Package
   b. Perceptual maps
   c. Supreme Court of the United States
   d. Value

9. In statistical hypothesis testing, the _____ formally describes some aspect of the statistical behaviour of a set of data; this description is treated as valid unless the actual behaviour of the data contradicts this assumption. Thus, the _____ is contrasted against another hypothesis. Statistical hypothesis testing is used to make a decision about whether the data contradicts the _____: this is called significance testing.
   a. Statistical hypothesis test
   b. Standard score
   c. Variance
   d. Null hypothesis

10. _____ is a computer program used for statistical analysis.

    _____ (originally, Statistical Package for the Social Sciences) was released in its first version in 1968 after being founded by Norman Nie and C. Hadlai Hull. Nie was then a political science postgraduate at Stanford University, and now Research Professor in the Department of Political Science at Stanford and Professor Emeritus of Political Science at the University of Chicago.

    a. SPSS
    b. Power III
    c. 6-3-5 Brainwriting
    d. 180SearchAssistant

11. _____ refer to a collection of facts usually collected as the result of experience, observation or experiment or a set of premises. This may consist of numbers, words particularly as measurements or observations of a set of variables. _____ are often viewed as a lowest level of abstraction from which information and knowledge are derived.
    a. Mean
    b. Sample size
    c. Pearson product-moment correlation coefficient
    d. Data

12. _____ is one of the four elements of marketing mix. An organization or set of organizations (go-betweens) involved in the process of making a product or service available for use or consumption by a consumer or business user.

The other three parts of the marketing mix are product, pricing, and promotion.

   a. Better Living Through Chemistry
   b. Comparison-Shopping agent
   c. Japan Advertising Photographers' Association
   d. Distribution

Chapter 16. Data Analysis: Testing for Association

13. In statistics, a _____ is a tabulation of the values that one or more variables take in a sample.

Univariate _____s are often presented as lists, ordered by quantity, showing the number of times each value appears. For example, if 100 people rate a five-point Likert scale assessing their agreement with a statement on a scale on which 1 denotes strong agreement and 5 strong disagreement, the _____ of their responses might look like:

This simple tabulation has two drawbacks.

- a. Frequency distribution
- b. Survey research
- c. Confidence interval
- d. Statistics

14. The _____ and the null hypothesis are the two rival hypotheses whose likelihoods are compared by a statistical hypothesis test. Usually the _____ is the possibility that an observed effect is genuine and the null hypothesis is the rival possibility that it has resulted from chance.

The classical (or frequentist) approach is to calculate the probability that the observed effect (or one more extreme) will occur if the null hypothesis is true.

- a. ACNielsen
- b. Alternative hypothesis
- c. Interval estimation
- d. Analysis of variance

15. In statistics, the _____, R^2 is used in the context of statistical models whose main purpose is the prediction of future outcomes on the basis of other related information. It is the proportion of variability in a data set that is accounted for by the statistical model. It provides a measure of how well future outcomes are likely to be predicted by the model.

- a. Multicollinearity
- b. Regression analysis
- c. Coefficient of determination
- d. Variance inflation factor

16. In probability theory and statistics, a _____ is described as the number separating the higher half of a sample, a population from the lower half. The _____ of a finite list of numbers can be found by arranging all the observations from lowest value to highest value and picking the middle one. If there is an even number of observations, the _____ is not unique, so one often takes the mean of the two middle values.

- a. Statistically significant
- b. Linear regression
- c. Median
- d. Frequency distribution

17. A _____ is a statement or claim that a particular event will occur in the future in more certain terms than a forecast. The etymology of this word is Latin . In regards to predicting the future Howard H. Stevenson Says, ' _____ is at least two things: Important and hard.' Important, because we have to act, and hard because we have to realize the future we want, and what is the best way to get there.

- a. 180SearchAssistant
- b. Prediction
- c. Power III
- d. 6-3-5 Brainwriting

18. The terms '_____' and 'independent variable' are used in similar but subtly different ways in mathematics and statistics as part of the standard terminology in those subjects. They are used to distinguish between two types of quantities being considered, separating them into those available at the start of a process and those being created by it, where the latter (_____s) are dependent on the former (independent variables.)

Chapter 16. Data Analysis: Testing for Association

In traditional calculus, a function is defined as a relation between two terms called variables because their values vary.

a. Dependent variable
b. Power III
c. Field experiment
d. 180SearchAssistant

19. A number of different _____s are indicated below.

- Randomized controlled trial
    - Double-blind randomized trial
    - Single-blind randomized trial
    - Non-blind trial
- Nonrandomized trial (quasi-experiment)
    - Interrupted time series design (measures on a sample or a series of samples from the same population are obtained several times before and after a manipulated event or a naturally occurring event) - considered a type of quasi-experiment

- Cohort study
    - Prospective cohort
    - Retrospective cohort
    - Time series study
- Case-control study
    - Nested case-control study
- Cross-sectional study
    - Community survey (a type of cross-sectional study)

When choosing a _____, many factors must be taken into account. Different types of studies are subject to different types of bias. For example, recall bias is likely to occur in cross-sectional or case-control studies where subjects are asked to recall exposure to risk factors.

a. Longitudinal studies
b. Power III
c. 180SearchAssistant
d. Study design

20. In statistics, _____ is used for two things;

- to construct a simple formula that will predict what value will occur for a quantity of interest when other related variables take given values.
- to allow a test to be made of whether a given variable does have an effect on a quantity of interest in situations where there may be many related variables.

In both cases, several sets of outcomes are available for the quantity of interest together with the related variables.

_____ is a form of regression analysis in which the relationship between one or more independent variables and another variable, called the dependent variable, is modelled by a least squares function, called a _____ equation. This function is a linear combination of one or more model parameters, called regression coefficients. A _____ equation with one independent variable represents a straight line when the predicted value (i.e. the dependant variable from the regression equation) is plotted against the independent variable: this is called a simple _____.

a. Sample size
c. Linear regression
b. Descriptive statistics
d. Heteroskedastic

21. In statistics, _____ is a collection of statistical models, and their associated procedures, in which the observed variance is partitioned into components due to different explanatory variables. The initial techniques of the _____ were developed by the statistician and geneticist R. A. Fisher in the 1920s and 1930s, and is sometimes known as Fisher's ANOVA or Fisher's _____, due to the use of Fisher's F-distribution as part of the test of statistical significance.

There are three conceptual classes of such models:

1. Fixed-effects models assumes that the data came from normal populations which may differ only in their means. (Model 1)
2. Random effects models assume that the data describe a hierarchy of different populations whose differences are constrained by the hierarchy. (Model 2)
3. Mixed-effect models describe situations where both fixed and random effects are present. (Model 3)

In practice, there are several types of ANOVA depending on the number of treatments and the way they are applied to the subjects in the experiment:

- One-way ANOVA is used to test for differences among two or more independent groups. Typically, however, the One-way ANOVA is used to test for differences among at least three groups, since the two-group case can be covered by a T-test (Gossett, 1908.)

a. Interval estimation
c. ACNielsen
b. Arithmetic mean
d. Analysis of variance

22. In probability theory and statistics, the _____ of a random variable, probability distribution, or sample is a measure of statistical dispersion, averaging the squared distance of its possible values from the expected value (mean.) Whereas the mean is a way to describe the location of a distribution, the _____ is a way to capture its scale or degree of being spread out. The unit of _____ is the square of the unit of the original variable.

a. Correlation
c. Sample size
b. Standard deviation
d. Variance

23. An example of a repeated measures _____ would be if one group were pre- and post-tested. (This example occurs in education quite frequently.) If a teacher wanted to examine the effect of a new set of textbooks on student achievement, (s)he could test the class at the beginning of the year (pretest) and at the end of the year (posttest.)

a. Statistically significant
b. T-test
c. Moving average
d. Null hypothesis

24. _____ is a statistical technique used in market research to determine how people value different features that make up an individual product or service.

The objective of _____ is to determine what combination of a limited number of attributes is most influential on respondent choice or decision making. A controlled set of potential products or services is shown to respondents and by analyzing how they make preferences between these products, the implicit valuation of the individual elements making up the product or service can be determined.

a. Semantic differential
b. Power III
c. Likert scale
d. Conjoint analysis

25. _____ is a statistical phenomenon in which two or more predictor variables in a multiple regression model are highly correlated. In this situation the coefficient estimates may change erratically in response to small changes in the model or the data. _____ does not reduce the predictive power or reliability of the model as a whole; it only affects calculations regarding individual predictors.

a. Stepwise regression
b. Regression analysis
c. Variance inflation factor
d. Multicollinearity

Chapter 17. Data Analysis: Multivariate Techniques for the Research Process

1. _____ refer to a collection of facts usually collected as the result of experience, observation or experiment or a set of premises. This may consist of numbers, words particularly as measurements or observations of a set of variables. _____ are often viewed as a lowest level of abstraction from which information and knowledge are derived.
   a. Sample size
   b. Data
   c. Pearson product-moment correlation coefficient
   d. Mean

2. _____ is the process of extracting hidden patterns from data. As more data is gathered, with the amount of data doubling every three years, _____ is becoming an increasingly important tool to transform this data into information. It is commonly used in a wide range of profiling practices, such as marketing, surveillance, fraud detection and scientific discovery.
   a. Structure mining
   b. 180SearchAssistant
   c. Power III
   d. Data mining

3. _____ is an advertisement in which a particular product specifically mentions a competitor by name for the express purpose of showing why the competitor is inferior to the product naming it.

This should not be confused with parody advertisements, where a fictional product is being advertised for the purpose of poking fun at the particular advertisement, nor should it be confused with the use of a coined brand name for the purpose of comparing the product without actually naming an actual competitor. ('Wikipedia tastes better and is less filling than the Encyclopedia Galactica.')

In the 1980s, during what has been referred to as the cola wars, soft-drink manufacturer Pepsi ran a series of advertisements where people, caught on hidden camera, in a blind taste test, chose Pepsi over rival Coca-Cola.

   a. Comparative advertising
   b. Heavy-up
   c. Cost per conversion
   d. GL-70

4. _____ is a graphics technique used by asset marketers that attempts to visually display the perceptions of customers or potential customers. Typically the position of a product, product line, brand, or company is displayed relative to their competition.

Perceptual maps can have any number of dimensions but the most common is two dimensions.

   a. Perceptual mapping
   b. Kano model
   c. Customer franchise
   d. Market environment

5. A _____ is a structured collection of records or data that is stored in a computer system. The structure is achieved by organizing the data according to a _____ model. The model in most common use today is the relational model.
   a. Power III
   b. 6-3-5 Brainwriting
   c. 180SearchAssistant
   d. Database

Chapter 17. Data Analysis: Multivariate Techniques for the Research Process 155

6. A _____, in the field of business and marketing, is a geographic region or demographic group used to gauge the viability of a product or service in the mass market prior to a wide scale roll-out. The criteria used to judge the acceptability of a _____ region or group include:

1. a population that is demographically similar to the proposed target market; and
2. relative isolation from densely populated media markets so that advertising to the test audience can be efficient and economical.

The _____ ideally aims to duplicate 'everything' - promotion and distribution as well as `product' - on a smaller scale. The technique replicates, typically in one area, what is planned to occur in a national launch; and the results are very carefully monitored, so that they can be extrapolated to projected national results. The `area' may be any one of the following:

- Television area
- Test town
- Residential neighborhood
- Test site

A number of decisions have to be taken about any _____:

- Which _____?
- What is to be tested?
- How long a test?
- What are the success criteria?

The simple go or no-go decision, together with the related reduction of risk, is normally the main justification for the expense of _____s. At the same time, however, such _____s can be used to test specific elements of a new product's marketing mix; possibly the version of the product itself, the promotional message and media spend, the distribution channels and the price.

a. Power III
b. 180SearchAssistant
c. Preadolescence
d. Test market

7. _____ is a type of research conducted because a problem has not been clearly defined. _____ helps determine the best research design, data collection method and selection of subjects. Given its fundamental nature, _____ often concludes that a perceived problem does not actually exist.

a. Intent scale translation
b. ACNielsen
c. IDDEA
d. Exploratory research

8. _____ is defined by the American _____ Association as the activity, set of institutions, and processes for creating, communicating, delivering, and exchanging offerings that have value for customers, clients, partners, and society at large. The term developed from the original meaning which referred literally to going to market, as in shopping, or going to a market to sell goods or services.

_____ practice tends to be seen as a creative industry, which includes advertising, distribution and selling.

Chapter 17. Data Analysis: Multivariate Techniques for the Research Process

a. Marketing
b. Customer acquisition management
c. Product naming
d. Marketing myopia

9. A number of different _____s are indicated below.

- Randomized controlled trial
    - Double-blind randomized trial
    - Single-blind randomized trial
    - Non-blind trial
- Nonrandomized trial (quasi-experiment)
    - Interrupted time series design (measures on a sample or a series of samples from the same population are obtained several times before and after a manipulated event or a naturally occurring event) - considered a type of quasi-experiment
- Cohort study
    - Prospective cohort
    - Retrospective cohort
    - Time series study
- Case-control study
    - Nested case-control study
- Cross-sectional study
    - Community survey (a type of cross-sectional study)

When choosing a _____, many factors must be taken into account. Different types of studies are subject to different types of bias. For example, recall bias is likely to occur in cross-sectional or case-control studies where subjects are asked to recall exposure to risk factors.

a. Longitudinal studies
b. Study design
c. 180SearchAssistant
d. Power III

10. A personal and cultural _____ is a relative ethic _____, an assumption upon which implementation can be extrapolated. A _____ system is a set of consistent _____s and measures that is soo not true. A principle _____ is a foundation upon which other _____s and measures of integrity are based.

a. Value
b. Supreme Court of the United States
c. Perceptual maps
d. Package-on-Package

11. _____ is a computer program used for statistical analysis.

_____ (originally, Statistical Package for the Social Sciences) was released in its first version in 1968 after being founded by Norman Nie and C. Hadlai Hull. Nie was then a political science postgraduate at Stanford University, and now Research Professor in the Department of Political Science at Stanford and Professor Emeritus of Political Science at the University of Chicago.

a. 180SearchAssistant
b. Power III
c. 6-3-5 Brainwriting
d. SPSS

Chapter 17. Data Analysis: Multivariate Techniques for the Research Process

12. The _____ and the null hypothesis are the two rival hypotheses whose likelihoods are compared by a statistical hypothesis test. Usually the _____ is the possibility that an observed effect is genuine and the null hypothesis is the rival possibility that it has resulted from chance.

The classical (or frequentist) approach is to calculate the probability that the observed effect (or one more extreme) will occur if the null hypothesis is true.

a. Interval estimation
b. Alternative hypothesis
c. Analysis of variance
d. ACNielsen

13. A _____ is a business that is independently owned and operated, with a small number of employees and relatively low volume of sales. The legal definition of 'small' often varies by country and industry, but is generally under 100 employees in the United States and under 50 employees in the European Union. In comparison, the definition of mid-sized business by the number of employees is generally under 500 in the U.S. and 250 for the European Union.

a. Product support
b. Time to market
c. Customer centricity
d. Small business

14. '_____' is a class of statistical techniques that can be applied to data that exhibit 'natural' groupings. _____ sorts through the raw data and groups them into clusters. A cluster is a group of relatively homogeneous cases or observations.

a. Cluster analysis
b. Structure mining
c. 180SearchAssistant
d. Power III

15. In algebra, the _____ of a polynomial with real or complex coefficients is a certain expression in the coefficients of the polynomial which is equal to zero if and only if the polynomial has a multiple root (i.e. a root with multiplicity greater than one) in the complex numbers. For example, the _____ of the quadratic polynomial

$$ax^2 + bx + c \text{ is } b^2 - 4ac.$$

The _____ of the cubic polynomial

$$ax^3 + bx^2 + cx + d \text{ is } b^2c^2 - 4ac^3 - 4b^3d - 27a^2d^2 + 18abcd.$$

a. Lifestyle center
b. Discriminant
c. Consumption Map
d. Flighting

16. Linear _____ and the related Fisher's linear discriminant are methods used in statistics and machine learning to find the linear combination of features which best separate two or more classes of objects or events. The resulting combination may be used as a linear classifier, or, more commonly, for dimensionality reduction before later classification.

LDiscriminant analysis is closely related to ANOVA (analysis of variance) and regression analysis, which also attempt to express one dependent variable as a linear combination of other features or measurements.

Chapter 17. Data Analysis: Multivariate Techniques for the Research Process

a. Discriminant analysis
c. Linear discriminant analysis
b. Multiple discriminant analysis
d. Geodemographic segmentation

17. _____ is a statistical method used to describe variability among observed variables in terms of fewer unobserved variables called factors. The observed variables are modeled as linear combinations of the factors, plus 'error' terms. The information gained about the interdependencies can be used later to reduce the set of variables in a dataset.
    a. Likert scale
    c. Power III
    b. Semantic differential
    d. Factor analysis

18. _____ is a set of related statistical techniques often used in information visualization for exploring similarities or dissimilarities in data. MDS is a special case of ordination. An MDS algorithm starts with a matrix of item-item similarities, then assigns a location to each item in N-dimensional space, where N is specified a priori.
    a. Cocooning
    c. Situational theory of publics
    b. Convenience
    d. Multidimensional scaling

19. In statistics, _____ is a generalization of linear discriminant analysis.
    a. Principal component analysis
    c. Discriminant analysis
    b. Linear discriminant analysis
    d. Multiple discriminant analysis

20. In statistics, _____ is used for two things;

    - to construct a simple formula that will predict what value will occur for a quantity of interest when other related variables take given values.
    - to allow a test to be made of whether a given variable does have an effect on a quantity of interest in situations where there may be many related variables.

In both cases, several sets of outcomes are available for the quantity of interest together with the related variables.

_____ is a form of regression analysis in which the relationship between one or more independent variables and another variable, called the dependent variable, is modelled by a least squares function, called a _____ equation. This function is a linear combination of one or more model parameters, called regression coefficients. A _____ equation with one independent variable represents a straight line when the predicted value (i.e. the dependant variable from the regression equation) is plotted against the independent variable: this is called a simple _____.

a. Descriptive statistics
c. Sample size
b. Linear regression
d. Heteroskedastic

21. In statistics, _____ is a collection of statistical models, and their associated procedures, in which the observed variance is partitioned into components due to different explanatory variables. The initial techniques of the _____ were developed by the statistician and geneticist R. A. Fisher in the 1920s and 1930s, and is sometimes known as Fisher's ANOVA or Fisher's _____, due to the use of Fisher's F-distribution as part of the test of statistical significance.

Chapter 17. Data Analysis: Multivariate Techniques for the Research Process

There are three conceptual classes of such models:

1. Fixed-effects models assumes that the data came from normal populations which may differ only in their means. (Model 1)
2. Random effects models assume that the data describe a hierarchy of different populations whose differences are constrained by the hierarchy. (Model 2)
3. Mixed-effect models describe situations where both fixed and random effects are present. (Model 3)

In practice, there are several types of ANOVA depending on the number of treatments and the way they are applied to the subjects in the experiment:

- One-way ANOVA is used to test for differences among two or more independent groups. Typically, however, the One-way ANOVA is used to test for differences among at least three groups, since the two-group case can be covered by a T-test (Gossett, 1908.)

a. Arithmetic mean
c. Interval estimation
b. ACNielsen
d. Analysis of variance

22. _____ is a statistical technique used in market research to determine how people value different features that make up an individual product or service.

The objective of _____ is to determine what combination of a limited number of attributes is most influential on respondent choice or decision making. A controlled set of potential products or services is shown to respondents and by analyzing how they make preferences between these products, the implicit valuation of the individual elements making up the product or service can be determined.

a. Power III
c. Semantic differential
b. Likert scale
d. Conjoint analysis

23. In statistics, _____ is a collective name for techniques for the modeling and analysis of numerical data consisting of values of a dependent variable and of one or more independent variables The dependent variable in the regression equation is modeled as a function of the independent variables, corresponding parameters, and an error term. The error term is treated as a random variable.

a. Stepwise regression
c. Variance inflation factor
b. Regression analysis
d. Multicollinearity

24. In probability theory and statistics, the _____ of a random variable, probability distribution, or sample is a measure of statistical dispersion, averaging the squared distance of its possible values from the expected value (mean.) Whereas the mean is a way to describe the location of a distribution, the _____ is a way to capture its scale or degree of being spread out. The unit of _____ is the square of the unit of the original variable.

a. Standard deviation
c. Correlation
b. Sample size
d. Variance

Chapter 17. Data Analysis: Multivariate Techniques for the Research Process

25. _____ is a process of gathering, modeling, and transforming data with the goal of highlighting useful information, suggesting conclusions, and supporting decision making. _____ has multiple facets and approaches, encompassing diverse techniques under a variety of names, in different business, science, and social science domains.

Data mining is a particular _____ technique that focuses on modeling and knowledge discovery for predictive rather than purely descriptive purposes.

   a. Power III
   b. 6-3-5 Brainwriting
   c. Data analysis
   d. 180SearchAssistant

26. _____ is one of the four elements of marketing mix. An organization or set of organizations (go-betweens) involved in the process of making a product or service available for use or consumption by a consumer or business user.

The other three parts of the marketing mix are product, pricing, and promotion.

   a. Comparison-Shopping agent
   b. Distribution
   c. Better Living Through Chemistry
   d. Japan Advertising Photographers' Association

27. _____ is a form of communication that typically attempts to persuade potential customers to purchase or to consume more of a particular brand of product or service. 'While now central to the contemporary global economy and the reproduction of global production networks, it is only quite recently that _____ has been more than a marginal influence on patterns of sales and production. The formation of modern _____ was intimately bound up with the emergence of new forms of monopoly capitalism around the end of the 19th and beginning of the 20th century as one element in corporate strategies to create, organize and where possible control markets, especially for mass produced consumer goods.

   a. Advertising
   b. ACNielsen
   c. ADTECH
   d. AMAX

28. _____ is a statistical phenomenon in which two or more predictor variables in a multiple regression model are highly correlated. In this situation the coefficient estimates may change erratically in response to small changes in the model or the data. _____ does not reduce the predictive power or reliability of the model as a whole; it only affects calculations regarding individual predictors.

   a. Regression analysis
   b. Stepwise regression
   c. Variance inflation factor
   d. Multicollinearity

29. In environmental modeling and especially in hydrology, a _____ model means a model that is acceptably consistent with observed natural processes, i.e. that simulates well, for example, observed river discharge. It is a key concept of the so-called Generalized Likelihood Uncertainty Estimation (GLUE) methodology to quantify how uncertain environmental predictions are.

   a. 6-3-5 Brainwriting
   b. Behavioral
   c. Power III
   d. 180SearchAssistant

30. A _____ applies the scientific method to experimentally examine an intervention in the real world (or as many experimental economists like to say, naturally-occurring environments) rather than in the laboratory. _____s, like lab experiments, generally randomize subjects (or other sampling units) into treatment and control groups and compare outcomes between these groups. Clinical trials of pharmaceuticals are one example of _____s.

a. Response variable
b. Power III
c. 180SearchAssistant
d. Field experiment

31. A _____ is a subgroup of people or organizations sharing one or more characteristics that cause them to have similar product and/or service needs. A true _____ meets all of the following criteria: it is distinct from other segments (different segments have different needs), it is homogeneous within the segment (exhibits common needs); it responds similarly to a market stimulus, and it can be reached by a market intervention. The term is also used when consumers with identical product and/or service needs are divided up into groups so they can be charged different amounts.
   a. Market segment
   b. Customer insight
   c. Commercial planning
   d. Production orientation

32. _____ in organizations and public policy is both the organizational process of creating and maintaining a plan; and the psychological process of thinking about the activities required to create a desired goal on some scale. As such, it is a fundamental property of intelligent behavior. This thought process is essential to the creation and refinement of a plan, or integration of it with other plans, that is, it combines forecasting of developments with the preparation of scenarios of how to react to them.
   a. 180SearchAssistant
   b. Power III
   c. 6-3-5 Brainwriting
   d. Planning

33. In statistics, a result is called _____ if it is unlikely to have occurred by chance. 'A _____ difference' simply means there is statistical evidence that there is a difference; it does not mean the difference is necessarily large, important, or significant in the common meaning of the word.

The significance level of a test is a traditional frequentist statistical hypothesis testing concept.

   a. Frequency distribution
   b. Standard deviation
   c. Statistically significant
   d. Randomization

34. _____ is the pioneer of the digital video recorder . _____ was introduced in the United States, and is now available in Canada, Mexico, Australia, and Taiwan. Created by _____, Inc..
   a. Power III
   b. 180SearchAssistant
   c. 6-3-5 Brainwriting
   d. TiVo

35. A _____ is a research instrument consisting of a series of questions and other prompts for the purpose of gathering information from respondents. Although they are often designed for statistical analysis of the responses, this is not always the case. The _____ was invented by Sir Francis Galton.
   a. Market research
   b. Mystery shopping
   c. Mystery shoppers
   d. Questionnaire

36. Consumer market research is a form of applied sociology that concentrates on understanding the behaviours, whims and preferences, of consumers in a market-based economy, and aims to understand the effects and comparative success of marketing campaigns. The field of consumer _____ as a statistical science was pioneered by Arthur Nielsen with the founding of the ACNielsen Company in 1923 .

162 *Chapter 17. Data Analysis: Multivariate Techniques for the Research Process*

Thus _____ is the systematic and objective identification, collection, analysis, and dissemination of information for the purpose of assisting management in decision making related to the identification and solution of problems and opportunities in marketing.

   a. Logit analysis   b. Marketing Research
   c. Marketing research process   d. Focus group

37. _____ is a broad label that refers to any individuals or households that use goods and services generated within the economy. The concept of a _____ is used in different contexts, so that the usage and significance of the term may vary.

A _____ is a person who uses any product or service.

   a. Consumer   b. Power III
   c. 6-3-5 Brainwriting   d. 180SearchAssistant

38. Human beings are also considered to be _____ because they have the ability to change raw materials into valuable _____. The term Human _____ can also be defined as the skills, energies, talents, abilities and knowledge that are used for the production of goods or the rendering of services. While taking into account human beings as _____, the following things have to be kept in mind:

- The size of the population
- The capabilities of the individuals in that population

Many _____ cannot be consumed in their original form. They have to be processed in order to change them into more usable commodities.

   a. Resources   b. 180SearchAssistant
   c. Power III   d. 6-3-5 Brainwriting

Chapter 18. Preparing the Marketing Research Report and Presentation

1. _____ is defined by the American _____ Association as the activity, set of institutions, and processes for creating, communicating, delivering, and exchanging offerings that have value for customers, clients, partners, and society at large. The term developed from the original meaning which referred literally to going to market, as in shopping, or going to a market to sell goods or services.

   _____ practice tends to be seen as a creative industry, which includes advertising, distribution and selling.

   a. Product naming
   b. Marketing myopia
   c. Customer acquisition management
   d. Marketing

2. A personal and cultural _____ is a relative ethic _____, an assumption upon which implementation can be extrapolated. A _____ system is a set of consistent _____ s and measures that is soo not true. A principle _____ is a foundation upon which other _____ s and measures of integrity are based.
   a. Value
   b. Supreme Court of the United States
   c. Package-on-Package
   d. Perceptual maps

3. _____ is a term used in business for a short document that summarises a longer report, proposal or group of related reports in such a way that readers can rapidly become acquainted with a large body of material without having to read it all. It will usually contain a brief statement of the problem or proposal covered in the major document(s), background information, concise analysis and main conclusions. It is intended as an aid to decision making by business managers.
   a. AMAX
   b. ACNielsen
   c. ADTECH
   d. Executive summary

4. _____ refer to a collection of facts usually collected as the result of experience, observation or experiment or a set of premises. This may consist of numbers, words particularly as measurements or observations of a set of variables. _____ are often viewed as a lowest level of abstraction from which information and knowledge are derived.
   a. Sample size
   b. Pearson product-moment correlation coefficient
   c. Mean
   d. Data

5. _____ is a process of gathering, modeling, and transforming data with the goal of highlighting useful information, suggesting conclusions, and supporting decision making. _____ has multiple facets and approaches, encompassing diverse techniques under a variety of names, in different business, science, and social science domains.

   Data mining is a particular _____ technique that focuses on modeling and knowledge discovery for predictive rather than purely descriptive purposes.

   a. Data analysis
   b. 6-3-5 Brainwriting
   c. Power III
   d. 180SearchAssistant

6. Consumer market research is a form of applied sociology that concentrates on understanding the behaviours, whims and preferences, of consumers in a market-based economy, and aims to understand the effects and comparative success of marketing campaigns. The field of consumer _____ as a statistical science was pioneered by Arthur Nielsen with the founding of the ACNielsen Company in 1923 .

   Thus _____ is the systematic and objective identification, collection, analysis, and dissemination of information for the purpose of assisting management in decision making related to the identification and solution of problems and opportunities in marketing.

a. Focus group
c. Logit analysis
b. Marketing research process
d. Marketing research

7. A _____ is a structured collection of records or data that is stored in a computer system. The structure is achieved by organizing the data according to a _____ model. The model in most common use today is the relational model.
   a. 180SearchAssistant
   c. 6-3-5 Brainwriting
   b. Power III
   d. Database

8. A _____, in the field of business and marketing, is a geographic region or demographic group used to gauge the viability of a product or service in the mass market prior to a wide scale roll-out. The criteria used to judge the acceptability of a _____ region or group include:

   1. a population that is demographically similar to the proposed target market; and
   2. relative isolation from densely populated media markets so that advertising to the test audience can be efficient and economical.

The _____ ideally aims to duplicate 'everything' - promotion and distribution as well as `product' - on a smaller scale. The technique replicates, typically in one area, what is planned to occur in a national launch; and the results are very carefully monitored, so that they can be extrapolated to projected national results. The `area' may be any one of the following:

- Television area
- Test town
- Residential neighborhood
- Test site

A number of decisions have to be taken about any _____:

- Which _____?
- What is to be tested?
- How long a test?
- What are the success criteria?

The simple go or no-go decision, together with the related reduction of risk, is normally the main justification for the expense of _____s. At the same time, however, such _____s can be used to test specific elements of a new product's marketing mix; possibly the version of the product itself, the promotional message and media spend, the distribution channels and the price.

   a. Power III
   c. 180SearchAssistant
   b. Preadolescence
   d. Test market

9. _____ is a type of research conducted because a problem has not been clearly defined. _____ helps determine the best research design, data collection method and selection of subjects. Given its fundamental nature, _____ often concludes that a perceived problem does not actually exist.

Chapter 18. Preparing the Marketing Research Report and Presentation

a. Intent scale translation
b. ACNielsen
c. IDDEA
d. Exploratory research

10. A number of different _____s are indicated below.

- Randomized controlled trial
    - Double-blind randomized trial
    - Single-blind randomized trial
    - Non-blind trial
- Nonrandomized trial (quasi-experiment)
    - Interrupted time series design (measures on a sample or a series of samples from the same population are obtained several times before and after a manipulated event or a naturally occurring event) - considered a type of quasi-experiment

- Cohort study
    - Prospective cohort
    - Retrospective cohort
    - Time series study
- Case-control study
    - Nested case-control study
- Cross-sectional study
    - Community survey (a type of cross-sectional study)

When choosing a _____, many factors must be taken into account. Different types of studies are subject to different types of bias. For example, recall bias is likely to occur in cross-sectional or case-control studies where subjects are asked to recall exposure to risk factors.

a. Study design
b. Power III
c. Longitudinal studies
d. 180SearchAssistant

11. A _____ is a form of qualitative research in which a group of people are asked about their attitude towards a product, service, concept, advertisement, idea, or packaging. Questions are asked in an interactive group setting where participants are free to talk with other group members.

Ernest Dichter originated the idea of having a 'group therapy' for products and this process is what became known as a _____.

a. Cross tabulation
b. Marketing research process
c. Focus group
d. Logit analysis

12. In statistics, the _____ is a common measure of the correlation (linear dependence) between two variables X and Y. It is very widely used in the sciences as a measure of the strength of linear dependence between two variables, giving a value somewhere between +1 and -1 inclusive. It was first introduced by Francis Galton in the 1880s, and named after Karl Pearson.

In accordance with the usual convention, when calculated for an entire population, the Pearson product-moment correlation is typically designated by the analogous Greek letter, which in this case is ρ .

   a. Pearson product-moment correlation coefficient   b. Control chart
   c. Standard deviation   d. Median

13. _____ is a computer program used for statistical analysis.

_____ (originally, Statistical Package for the Social Sciences) was released in its first version in 1968 after being founded by Norman Nie and C. Hadlai Hull. Nie was then a political science postgraduate at Stanford University, and now Research Professor in the Department of Political Science at Stanford and Professor Emeritus of Political Science at the University of Chicago.

   a. 6-3-5 Brainwriting   b. Power III
   c. 180SearchAssistant   d. SPSS

14. In probability theory and statistics, _____ indicates the strength and direction of a linear relationship between two random variables. That is in contrast with the usage of the term in colloquial speech, denoting any relationship, not necessarily linear. In general statistical usage, _____ or co-relation refers to the departure of two random variables from independence.
   a. Mean   b. Probability
   c. Frequency distribution   d. Correlation

15. In statistics, _____ is a collective name for techniques for the modeling and analysis of numerical data consisting of values of a dependent variable and of one or more independent variables The dependent variable in the regression equation is modeled as a function of the independent variables, corresponding parameters, and an error term. The error term is treated as a random variable.
   a. Stepwise regression   b. Multicollinearity
   c. Variance inflation factor   d. Regression analysis

ANSWER KEY

Chapter 1
1. d   2. d   3. b   4. b   5. c   6. c   7. d   8. c   9. d   10. b
11. d   12. c   13. a   14. b   15. a   16. d   17. d   18. a   19. d   20. c
21. b   22. d   23. b   24. d   25. b   26. d   27. d   28. d   29. b   30. d
31. d   32. d   33. d   34. a   35. d   36. d   37. d   38. d   39. a   40. d
41. d   42. a   43. d   44. a   45. c   46. a   47. d   48. b   49. a   50. d
51. d   52. d   53. b   54. d   55. d   56. a   57. d   58. c   59. d   60. b
61. a   62. d   63. c   64. c   65. d   66. a   67. c   68. a   69. d   70. a
71. d   72. d   73. d   74. a   75. d   76. a   77. c   78. d   79. b   80. d
81. b   82. d   83. b   84. d   85. d   86. b   87. d   88. b   89. c   90. a
91. d

Chapter 2
1. a   2. d   3. a   4. b   5. b   6. d   7. d   8. a   9. d   10. d
11. d   12. d   13. b   14. a   15. d   16. d   17. c   18. d   19. d   20. c
21. d   22. d   23. a   24. b   25. d   26. d   27. d   28. a   29. b   30. d
31. c   32. d   33. a   34. a   35. b   36. d   37. d   38. b   39. a   40. d
41. d   42. d   43. c   44. a   45. d   46. d   47. c

Chapter 3
1. d   2. d   3. c   4. a   5. d   6. d   7. d   8. c   9. c   10. d
11. d   12. d   13. d   14. c   15. d   16. d   17. b   18. d   19. d   20. b
21. d   22. d   23. a   24. d   25. c   26. b   27. d   28. d   29. d   30. b
31. d   32. b   33. c   34. d   35. c   36. d   37. a   38. d   39. d   40. a
41. a   42. c   43. b   44. d   45. d   46. b   47. d   48. b   49. d   50. d
51. a   52. d   53. d   54. d   55. d   56. a

Chapter 4
1. a   2. d   3. d   4. d   5. c   6. d   7. a   8. c   9. b   10. a
11. d   12. a   13. c   14. a   15. d   16. b   17. d   18. d   19. a   20. d
21. d   22. d   23. d   24. b   25. d   26. b   27. d   28. a   29. d   30. a
31. d   32. c   33. d   34. d   35. d   36. d   37. d   38. c   39. d

Chapter 5
1. a   2. b   3. d   4. b   5. c   6. c   7. a   8. d   9. d   10. d
11. d   12. d   13. c   14. a   15. a   16. d   17. a   18. d   19. d   20. c
21. c   22. c   23. d   24. d   25. d   26. d   27. d   28. b   29. d   30. b
31. c   32. c   33. c   34. d   35. a   36. d   37. c   38. a   39. d   40. b
41. b   42. a   43. d   44. c   45. a

Chapter 6
1. d   2. b   3. b   4. d   5. d   6. d   7. b   8. d   9. d   10. d
11. d   12. b   13. d   14. d   15. c   16. d   17. b   18. d   19. b   20. a
21. d   22. a   23. d   24. b   25. d   26. d   27. a   28. a   29. b   30. d
31. c   32. a   33. d   34. d   35. b   36. c   37. b   38. b   39. d   40. c
41. d   42. d   43. d   44. d

Chapter 7
1. c	2. d	3. d	4. d	5. d	6. a	7. d	8. d	9. d	10. d
11. d	12. d	13. d	14. d	15. b	16. d	17. a	18. d	19. d	20. d
21. c	22. d	23. a	24. a	25. d	26. b	27. d	28. d	29. d	30. d
31. b	32. a	33. b	34. a	35. d	36. b	37. c	38. d	39. b	40. a
41. a	42. d	43. d	44. c	45. c	46. d	47. d	48. a	49. d	50. c
51. c	52. a								

Chapter 8
1. d	2. d	3. d	4. d	5. d	6. b	7. d	8. a	9. a	10. d
11. d	12. d	13. d	14. c	15. b	16. d	17. d	18. d	19. b	20. a
21. d	22. c	23. d	24. c	25. d	26. d	27. d	28. b	29. b	30. c
31. d	32. c	33. d	34. d	35. c	36. a	37. b	38. c	39. a	40. c
41. d	42. b	43. c	44. b	45. d	46. d				

Chapter 9
1. d	2. d	3. d	4. d	5. c	6. d	7. d	8. d	9. d	10. b
11. c	12. d	13. d	14. a	15. b	16. b	17. d	18. d	19. d	20. d
21. c	22. d	23. d	24. d	25. a	26. b	27. c	28. c	29. d	30. b
31. c	32. d	33. a	34. d	35. d	36. d	37. d	38. d	39. d	40. b

Chapter 10
1. b	2. d	3. a	4. d	5. d	6. d	7. d	8. d	9. a	10. d
11. d	12. b	13. d	14. d	15. d	16. d	17. d	18. d	19. c	20. d
21. b	22. d	23. d	24. d	25. c	26. b	27. d	28. b	29. d	30. d
31. d	32. c	33. a	34. c	35. b					

Chapter 11
1. d	2. b	3. d	4. d	5. a	6. d	7. d	8. d	9. d	10. d
11. a	12. d	13. a	14. a	15. d	16. d	17. d	18. b	19. d	20. c
21. d	22. d	23. d	24. d	25. c	26. d	27. d	28. b	29. c	30. d

Chapter 12
1. d	2. d	3. a	4. a	5. a	6. d	7. a	8. d	9. c	10. a
11. d	12. c	13. b	14. b	15. b	16. b	17. b	18. a	19. d	20. b
21. d	22. d	23. a	24. d	25. d	26. d	27. b	28. d	29. b	30. d
31. d	32. c	33. d	34. a						

Chapter 13
1. a	2. b	3. d	4. c	5. c	6. b	7. d	8. a	9. a	10. d
11. d	12. a	13. d	14. c	15. d	16. a	17. b	18. d	19. d	20. a
21. d	22. b	23. d	24. c	25. c	26. d	27. d	28. c		

ANSWER KEY

Chapter 14
1. d 2. d 3. a 4. b 5. a 6. a 7. b 8. d 9. b 10. a
11. d 12. d 13. d 14. a 15. d 16. d 17. c 18. d 19. c 20. d
21. d 22. c

Chapter 15
1. d 2. c 3. b 4. b 5. d 6. c 7. d 8. b 9. d 10. a
11. d 12. a 13. d 14. b 15. d 16. d 17. d 18. c 19. d 20. c
21. c 22. d 23. c 24. d 25. b 26. b 27. d 28. d 29. d 30. c
31. a 32. d 33. d 34. a 35. d 36. d 37. d 38. d 39. d 40. a
41. d 42. d 43. d

Chapter 16
1. d 2. b 3. b 4. a 5. c 6. d 7. d 8. d 9. d 10. a
11. d 12. d 13. a 14. b 15. c 16. c 17. b 18. a 19. d 20. c
21. d 22. d 23. b 24. d 25. d

Chapter 17
1. b 2. d 3. a 4. a 5. d 6. d 7. d 8. a 9. b 10. a
11. d 12. b 13. d 14. a 15. b 16. a 17. d 18. d 19. d 20. b
21. d 22. d 23. b 24. d 25. c 26. b 27. a 28. d 29. b 30. d
31. a 32. d 33. c 34. d 35. d 36. b 37. a 38. a

Chapter 18
1. d 2. a 3. d 4. d 5. a 6. d 7. d 8. d 9. d 10. a
11. c 12. a 13. d 14. d 15. d

www.ingramcontent.com/pod-product-compliance
Lightning Source LLC
Chambersburg PA
CBHW082204230426
43672CB00015B/2889